D0035296

NO LONGER PROPERTY OF
SEATTLE PUBLIC LIBRARY

More Praise for *Why Be Happy?*

"Scott Haas's insightful and engrossing exploration into the Japanese way of acceptance is a road map to a more meaningful life. This wonderful book excites with food for thought that is sumptuous, savory, and nuanced."

—Drew Nieporent, Restaurateur:
Nobu, Tribeca Grill, Bâtard

Why Be Happy?

Why Be Happy?

The Japanese Way of Acceptance

SCOTT HAAS

Go

hachette
BOOKS
New York

Copyright © 2020 by Scott Haas

Jacket design by Amanda Kain
Jacket illustration © Exotic_jp/Getty Images
Cover copyright © 2020 by Hachette Book Group, Inc.
Interior illustrations: © Exotic_jp/Getty Images; © seamartini/Getty Images

Hachette Book Group supports the right to free expression and the value of copyright. The purpose of copyright is to encourage writers and artists to produce the creative works that enrich our culture.

The scanning, uploading, and distribution of this book without permission is a theft of the author's intellectual property. If you would like permission to use material from the book (other than for review purposes), please contact permissions @hbgusa.com. Thank you for your support of the author's rights.

Hachette Go, an imprint of Hachette Books
Hachette Book Group
1290 Avenue of the Americas
New York, NY 10104
HachetteGo.com
Facebook.com/HachetteGo
Instagram.com/HachetteGo

First Edition: July 2020

Hachette Books is a division of Hachette Book Group, Inc.

The Hachette Go and Hachette Books name and logos are trademarks of Hachette Book Group, Inc.

The publisher is not responsible for websites (or their content) that are not owned by the publisher.

Print book interior design by Trish Wilkinson

Library of Congress Cataloging-in-Publication Data has been applied for.

ISBNs: 978-0-7382-8549-8 (hardcover), 978-0-7382-8551-1 (ebook), 978-0-306-92380-7 (international trade paperback)

Printed in the United States of America

LSC-C

10 9 8 7 6 5 4 3 2 1

For Dr. Reto Dürler, my oldest friend. A person whose passion for nature—from his knowledge of birds to his interest in the Swiss mountains—informs my thinking, deepens my awareness, and adds to my understanding. And, of course, for telling me about Braunwald: Hoch über dem Alltag.

I may live on until
I long for this time
as I remember now
unhappy times in the past
with fondness

ながらへば
またこの頃や
しのばれむ
憂しと見し世ぞ
今は恋しき

—Fujiwara No Kiyosuke, twelfth century

(translation by Yumi Obinata)

Translator's Note: The poem is one of the hundred poems
we memorize in order to play a traditional card game called
Hyakunin-isshu ("One Hundred Poems").

Contents

Why Be Happy?

Chapter
One

The World

Wait, what? Japan? What does Japan have to teach us about happiness?

A lot, as it turns out, and that's something that took me years to figure out, and I'm still puzzled and trying to make sense of it all. Key matters led me astray from the way I was brought up to think about happiness.

In Japan, happiness isn't a private experience. And happiness isn't really a goal. Acceptance is the goal.

What Japan does *at its best*, and what we can learn from its culture, is how to ward off the pain of being alone in the world. Accepting reality, past and present, and embracing things that don't last are fundamental to life in Japan. Spending time in Japan, studying its culture, and trying hard to figure out how people there go about planning, organizing, loving, and seeing themselves and nature have changed how I see and deal with stress.

Not everyone succeeds at being part of the multitude of groups in Japan, and isolation is a famous problem, as it is in the West with the elderly, the marginalized, and those with chronic mental illness.

But there are huge differences. Options exist for inclusion in Japan, from communal bathing to safe public parks to huge shrines and temples throughout the country that are open to all. A lot of mingling goes on (since the Taisho era, 1912–1926, but not before), thanks in part to Westernization that broke down barriers and hegemonies. Groups are central to existence from very early ages with kids all dressing the same and eating the exact same school lunches. Expectations are so obvious and widespread that a lot goes unspoken: you know how you are supposed to behave in Japan at home, in school, in shops, in restaurants, and at work—and these expectations don't vary much from person to person (although biases about gender and age and homogeneity are embedded and inhibiting).

Most of all, who you are as a human being in Japan, your self-identity, is formed as much by your group affiliations as by your quirks, opinions, and likes and dislikes.

Growing up in the United States, I adhere to our broad cultural opportunities: the "can do" spirit, the message of "Yes, I can," the extraordinary openness and creativity, the willingness to try new approaches to get things done, *the ferocity of individualism.*

This is where Japan comes in.

Observation, listening, being silent, taking things in, considering problems as *challenges*, being far less reactive, and, above all, practicing acceptance: these are at the pinnacle of how you relate to yourself and others. While these behaviors all exist elsewhere, of course, as they are characteristic of our species, in Japan they are the cornerstones of institutional and systemic development.

Knowing that who I am has a lot to do with who am I *with* is liberating. The road to self-analysis and self-satisfaction is endless, ironically confining, and peculiarly isolating.

Who needs privilege when you can have affiliation?

No place has added greater balance to my life, calm, patience, respect for silence and observation, and acceptance of how community and nature matter more than one's needs. The individualism we prize in the West is *supplemented* by an awareness that life's greatest pleasures come from satisfying others.

When others suffer, and we are empathic, our well-being is diminished. By this I mean: when we exercise our empathy, it implies absorbing the pain of others. As a clinician, when I hear, for example, terrifying narratives of loss, shame, and isolation, my well-being is diminished. This explains, in large part, why those suffering in ways evident to others are often shunned, blamed, or feared. The more we empathize with the pain of others, the more we recognize that their condition is part of our identity.

Think of it in the most pragmatic ways: if your child, spouse, parent, or dear friend is suffering, your well-being, because you feel part of them, and because they are in your heart and consciousness, is diminished. If my son or daughter or wife is suffering, I can't think about being happy.

Quite capable of creating my own stress, rather skilled at it, in fact, and coming from a family where stress was wholly normalized, I have had a tendency to repeat the same familiar mistakes.

And it's not just the personal. It never is—how could it be?

When I interview people at my job three mornings a week at the Department of Transitional Assistance in Dudley Square,* Roxbury, Massachusetts, doing disability evaluations among the homeless or impoverished or abused or recently incarcerated, and then drive back to my tony neighborhood, which is only five miles away, I can see in very stark relief that achievement and safety have far less to do with personal drive than with race, gender, and economics.

I found the help I needed, found what was missing, by integrating experiences in Japan with my life here.

Incorporating habits from Japan, gradually or even piecemeal, has fundamentally changed how I see and experience stress, how I avoid it, and how I accept the world while simultaneously trying hard to change my position in it.

Pushing the World Away is the name of one of jazz saxophonist Kenny Garrett's albums, and since he knows Japanese and has spent a lot of time in Japan, the title is an indication of how he and others, like me, view its culture.

---

*The name was changed to Nubian Square on December 19, 2019.

When I spoke to Garrett, he told me: "Japan has always been my second home." Inspired by Japanese culture, he said, "My music is pulling you in, pulling you in, pulling you in, pulling you in. The energy that we're using to push the world away is energy we can use in positive ways."

That's Japanese acceptance in a nutshell. Pushing the world away in a fervent approach to creating meaningful experiences that bring us closer to one another and to the sensuality of being alive.

Through integrating uncomplicated and daily activities and practices from Japan, I feel less stress that comes about from my own history as well as in working with the disenfranchised, whose stories are deeply cutting. It's an ongoing process; some days are better than others. And for sure I have more to work with than ever before, thanks to using observation, silence, and, above all, acceptance in its many facets. I have more ways to understand and decrease the destructive power of stress.

These aren't secrets to happiness; this isn't a way out of the challenges we face as human beings who are responsible citizens. It is a different way of seeing things, to paraphrase John Berger, adding to our current outlooks.* That way offers possibilities.

A while back, the idea of *ikigai* got really popular and was put forward as a code or secret that once you learned it, you would be well on your way to happiness. But Japan isn't just

---

* *Ways of Seeing* is a book about perception and art by the critic and novelist John Berger (1926–2017).

about happiness. More so, the Japanese story is fortitude, resilience, and community.*

What Japan offers is truly and fundamentally different ways of getting things done, seeing ourselves as part of nature, creating and being of use to communities, and accepting our very brief time here.

Just to be clear: Japanese have not cornered the market on empathy. Far from it. On a day-to-day basis, life in Japan is often characterized by indifference—people don't seem to want to react to others around them. *What if I say or do the*

---

* In his terrific book *What Makes Life Worth Living? How Japanese and Americans Make Sense of Their Worlds*, Gordon Mathews, an anthropologist at the Chinese University of Hong Kong, wrote, "The dominant meanings of *ikigai* are *ittaikan* and *jito jitsugen*, 'commitment to group,' and, 'self-realization.'" The idea is that self-realization comes about through positive experiences with others.

The *Japan Times*, in a review of the book that helped to spark the excitement, *Ikigai: The Japanese Secret to a Long and Happy Life*, by Héctor Garcia and Francesc Miralles, described *ikigai* as "the idea that having a purpose in your life is key to happiness." The reviewer writes, "Curious whether *ikigai* and longevity have a causal connection, software engineer Hector Garcia and writer/translator Francesc Miralles set out to interview the residents of Ogimi, Okinawa, the so-called Village of Longevity. Their resulting book claims that *ikigai* is 'The Japanese Secret to a Long and Happy Life.'" "It's an assertion the book fails to live up to," the *Japan Times* reviewer writes. "They don't connect *ikigai* with longevity in any convincing way. Instead the book is a patchwork of platitudes about diet and exercise, broken by interviews with centenarians and discussions of trends in psychotherapy. Their conclusion is correlation passed off as causation; the book is self-help painted as pseudo-philosophy." Numerous other books have shown up in recent years celebrating *ikigai* and suggesting that this is it—this is the key to well-being. Not exactly.

wrong thing? What if I am interfering? What will others think of me?

At the same time, *typically* (but not always) there is extraordinary public safety and civility established through powerful and overriding cohesion that has been well-established, in many ways, since day one. External structures are there to provide what is needed; the individual doesn't *have* to react much. Things are taken care of.

However, when a crisis does occur, one in which the external structures are not enough to solve matters, what is the individual supposed to do? Conditioned to look to the group for meaning, it can be difficult to know how to act and what to do.

My favorite artistic example of this takes place in *High and Low*, the 1963 Akira Kurosawa movie in which a wealthy Tokyo industrialist is forced to choose between being ruined in business or saving the life of the child of his chauffeur.

Putting aside his selfishness, which the movie suggests he acquired through postwar Americanization of Japan, the character Kingo Gondo (played by Toshiro Mifune) demonstrates that empathy trumps profit.

The movie was made when Japan was going into high gear—accelerating its industries, not just catching up with the West, but on the verge of surpassing it. Kurosawa was making the claim that the core values of Japanese culture were threatened by succumbing to Western concepts of success.

What, he wondered, was being lost?

The movie implies that empathy is the essence of Japanese culture and must not be sacrificed by adopting Western values driven by selfish greed. To help others, to understand and accept that we are part of a community: that's what Kurosawa is saying it means to be Japanese. In his view, selfishness and greed are temptations imposed by the Americans that must be rejected.

I know—it's a nationalistic movie!

Yet, in the United States, selflessness and empathy can be found everywhere. Whether through religious ties, community values, supportive and thoughtful families, or just a natural inclination to be caring, Americans think of ways each day to help others.

Jackie Robinson said, "A life is not important except in the impact it has on other lives."

The solitude, the separation we have from one another, the separation we have from nature, the selfishness that informs life all too often: these stressful concerns are addressed in Japan from a very early age.

Being part of family, school, company, and community is reinforced in Japan through a ton of everyday activities, behaviors, and ways of relating to one another, from observing to listening to apologizing (a lot!) to *accepting*.

The *han* (groups) of elementary schools, public bathing, unspoken relatedness, and public decorum are part of that effort or consensus. When individuals in Japan participate in each of these settings, their individualism is shaped by those around them. In a school, students must conform with uniforms and lunches. In public baths, naked among strangers or people recognizable from the community, privacy is no longer possible. The silence in crowds on sidewalks suggests that everyone is joined together (like it or not). All of these cultural representations and accepted behaviors lead to a shared sense of responsibility evident in healthy behaviors, highly functional communities, a great public infrastructure, and long life.*

No guarantees, but for sure thinking more about others and observing your surroundings leads to awareness: you're not alone and not that important—which should be a relief. Well-being comes from helping others and fitting in.

The ideal of community remains a mainstay and a function of Japan's cultural imperatives. Its goals are embedded in the faith that being part of a group is more important than asserting one's individuality. Asserting oneself—making individual demands that are not expressed by the group—is frowned upon in Japanese culture.

I've been fortunate to have Japanese friends whose patience with me, and ability to laugh at my numerous mistakes, has deepened my awareness. Japan is by far the most

---

*In the book *What Makes Life Worth Living?* Mathews describes the importance of *shudan seikatsu*, which he translates as "group living," in developing empathic qualities through social connections. Thomas Rohlen's classic and wonderful book, *Japan's High Schools*, is essential to what Mathews is writing, and so Mathews provides a generous quote from that work: "If we look closely at the developmental cycle, we find at every stage from nursery school to early employment the same basic routines reiterated and the same social lessons repeated time and again. Shared housekeeping chores, dress codes, group discussions, patterns of group assembly, and movement . . . are relearned at each new entry point. . . . Emphasis is always on standardizing the basic practices and understanding their moral implications in the context of *shudan seikatsu*."

relationship-driven country I've ever been to, a place where whom you are working with exceeds contractual matters.

Japan is also very didactic. Friends constantly correct me and take the time to show me the right way to do things. Whether it's how to hand someone a business card, what to ask at the outset of a meeting with a new colleague, or how to behave on a train, I've been taught how better to fit in.

Countless experiences from my early years visiting Japan for work attest to the guidance provided.

I first went to Niigata, a prefecture northwest of Tokyo, on the Sea of Japan, around 2005. I had told Rocky Aoki, the former Olympic wrestler and the founder of the enormously successful Benihana franchise, that I was headed there and asked him what to expect. He laughingly called it "the Oklahoma of Japan." Our conversation was taking place in Rocky's plush digs on Fifth Avenue in Manhattan, overlooking St. Patrick's Cathedral, and as far as he was concerned, Niigata was the provinces.

"Nothing to worry about," Rocky advised. "Full of hayseeds!"

It was anything but that. Sophisticated, rebuilt top to bottom since the war, and a no-nonsense kind of place, Niigata is like a great industrial city in the United States.

Fortunately, my friend Takeshi Endo, who had invited me to his city, tagged along to make sure I behaved myself properly. I had been hired by the sake brewers' association of the prefecture, many of whom Takeshi knew through his food company, to help introduce their beverages to the United States. Niigata sake, in case you're wondering, is regarded as some of the best in Japan because of the purity of the water that comes from the annual, massive snowfall.*

Anyway . . .

Takeshi literally stood at my elbow and told me how to hand out my *meishi* (business card), how to accept the card of the person I was meeting, how to look at the card, what to say after receiving the card, and where to put the card after receiving it.

"Tell him that you are grateful to be invited," he whispered in my ear. "Describe your hotel in favorable terms. Mention that you appreciate his trust in you."

Some of what he told me was not exactly unique to Japan, but what was different, and essential, was the precision and timing of the paces he was putting me through. And the clear implication that there were no alternatives: there was one right way to do things. I loved the clarity—what a relief! It was like scaffolding.

I had to look at the card and recite the person's name and occupation on it while looking briefly into his or her eyes. I had to say something along the lines of how impressed I was with the occupation. Then the person did the same with my card. After that, each card had to be pinched at the bottom corners, lined up to the exact measure of the table's edges, and placed facing the person who received it,

---

*The only sake served at NOBU, the famous restaurant in Manhattan, comes from one brewer located on Sado Island, which is part of Niigata prefecture. I wish this was product placement, but it's not, so when we celebrated my son Nick's eighteenth birthday there, it was on our dime, as it should be.

name and occupation showing. Takeshi and I had discussed the pauses between my questions and statements earlier that day: where to sit at a business meeting, where to stand in an elevator, whether to bow, how deep to bow, to shake hands or not shake hands.

My friends knew all these things the same way I knew how to tie my shoes; it gave structure and rhythm to the day. In Tokyo, Yuko told me how to order noodles at a shop: where to stand, how to line up, where to put coins in a machine at the entrance that issued tickets for each selection, which I handed to the host or hostess, who brought them to the cooks. Shinji instructed me on what phrases to say when thanking a chef after a meal. Yumi showed me what to do when exiting a restaurant and the staff are on the sidewalk waving goodbye and bowing until they can no longer see us. Jiro indicated where to sit in a car and what compliment to give a farmer who was showing us ducks that ate the bugs that had been destroying his rice.

As Jiro and I exited an Irish tea room, in the middle of nowhere in Ishikawa prefecture, the shop a perfect facsimile created by the deep pockets and fanaticism of the owner, who had brought over furniture and carpenters from Ireland, I was told: "Tell him he has a beautiful suit."

More about each one of these individuals later in the book.

What the endless catechism in Japan provides is a set of cozy honorifics that add confidence and affiliation. It's actually like a huge collection of secret handshakes. And once you get into the swing of it, it is reassuring and a great way of letting go of a lot of personal hang-ups.

Mind you, as a foreigner, I'm the entertainment. People are observing. Whether I get it wrong or right, it can be fun for the locals. Like the time in a restaurant when I folded the wrapper of my chopsticks into a tiny accordion on which to place the chopsticks.

Takeshi laughed.

"What's so funny?"

"A Japanese woman taught you that," he said.

"Oh?"

"A Japanese guy would never do that."

"So?"

"No problem," he said, and laughed again. "Just saying."

Or when I get it right and nail the honorifics, in an email or a speech at an *izakaya* that I've been asked to give rather suddenly to thank the host, a friend will whisper: "You sound so Japanese!"

Um, thanks, I guess.

In-groups, out-groups, ways to tell who's who. I really love it applied here—when the effort to affiliate comes *from* me *toward* another individual. To try hard to find what we have in common and build on that until we both feel safe with one another.

Like talking about the calming effect of watching ducks swim on a pond with a guy I'm evaluating who just got out of state prison after serving a decade for attempted murder. Or talking about favorite stew recipes with a woman in a scattered site shelter* for victims of domestic violence and how cooking gives her a sense of being at peace.

I'm not ignoring the tragedies or the antisocial behaviors, and I'm not minimizing the upheaval in their wake. I'm trying to build trust and see what we have in common as human beings long before anything else. I'm not into the pathology-driven approach to maladies.

It's better to start with what we have in common as healthy human beings, which, as it turns out, is far more than what we don't have in common.

These are *starting* points—based on affiliation—not the end points, and it's Japanese awareness of groups and my desire to inculcate them into my life here that has calmed me down a lot, brought me closer to others, and turned life into a set of observations rather than anything I used to react to in ways more personal.

At times, I pretend I'm in a movie:

The Airport. The Supermarket. Stuck in Traffic. On Hold with the Appliance Company.

When I see myself as part of a group that is in each of these situations, rather than going it alone, I'm better able to step back. And feel part of things as well as observe.

The groups are there if we bother to look for them and accept being part of them. We have more in common with that person on the margins than we may care to acknowledge.

---

*A scattered site shelter typically provides safe, temporary housing for homeless individuals with children.

And since I see and hear and feel aspects of that person that remind me of my family, past and present, I'm more inclined to do something to be of use to that individual. That is very satisfying.

The daily habits, the *very* pragmatic matters, make Japan a place where individuals are encouraged (and at times *required*) to let go of selfish needs and be part of their surroundings. When it works, you realize your insignificance, experience relationships and nature more fully, and focus on the needs of others. All this adds up to a deepening sense of satisfaction and well-being.

I hope to share with you the way of life in Japan that contributes to *ukeireru*—acceptance.

What does it mean to accept a state of letting go and put others' needs before yours? Japan is not the only country that prioritizes selflessness, but it is a place that uses this concept to inform how it structures and maintains institutions and systems.

In the West, letting go of self is epitomized in the poet John Keats's "doctrine of negative capability": "If a sparrow comes before my window, I take part in its existence and pick about the gravel . . . [so] that in a little time I am annihilated."

Now wait. Before you say, "Who in their right mind would want to be annihilated?," please remember a few facts: Keats died two hundred years ago, in 1821, at age twenty-five of tuberculosis. He was annihilated by mycobacteria, folks, not by a little bird. What he meant, what I mean, and what Japanese excel at is the annihilation of self-exploration, self-doubt, and pure selfishness.

It turns out that we are not our own best friends.

By observing nature and focusing on the immediate and transient, we get out of our heads, which is enormously relaxing.

In Japan, *that's a way of life.*

Chapter
Two

Acceptance

In Japan, numerous words mean "acceptance." Depending on who you are with and the situation in which you find yourself, finding the right words to express acceptance varies and presents challenges for the speaker and listener.

It's no different from countless Japanese words and phrases that function as symbols or representations of meanings.*

When deciding to write this book, I contacted friends in Japan to see if they could help me understand acceptance at deeper levels than my own—an outsider to their upbringings, culture, traditions, and history.

What might acceptance mean in Japan?

---

*Roland Barthes noted in *Empire of Signs*, his book about Japan, that meanings are not fixed and that the fluidity of words gives texts depth. Understanding the language is therefore often more of an interpretive process than a set of fixed absolutes. This may be why trust in relationships is so much in the foreground of negotiations in Japan, more than the content of the exchange, because while the content is open to interpretation, the relationship is less so: either you trust the person, or you don't. The language is not quite as reliable.

Yumi Obinata, an interpreter in Tokyo, sent me a highly detailed spreadsheet listing four words that mean acceptance. She then explained in what kind of sentence each word can be used and how to use them.

"*Ukeireru* is used by a mother with a child to accept something gently.

"*Uketomeru* is used by a mother to accept 'the burst of emotions of her child' when 'something comes with great force.'

"*Toriireru* can be used in describing the acceptance by Japan of Protestant missionaries.

"*Ukenagasu* can mean to receive and 'let it flow away.'"

Yumi explained further: "It is like if you are standing in a stream, you would rather stand sideways so that the water pressure on your body feels lighter. So here in Japan people accept disasters as part of life and try to *ukenagasu* so that they may not be affected too much psychologically.

"*Kikinagasu* can mean to hear and listen and let it flow away, meaning that we pretend to listen to somebody's nagging but not take it really seriously!

"*Juyo-Suro* can be used to describe accepting modern Western thoughts and systems."

Yumi said that "*jyō* can be six different words, and *ukeireru* is used often in day-to-day speech."

I have known Yumi and her family for many years. I've enjoyed talking to her son Nozomi about his college thesis on European Jewish post-Holocaust philosophers when he lived with my wife and me for a couple of weeks, having dinner with her and her husband and my wife in an upscale *izakaya* in Ginza, and drinking green tea with Yumi in Shimoda, the village in Shizuoka prefecture where the infamous black ships arrived in July 1853, with an ultimatum from Mathew Perry (the commodore, not the guy from *Friends*) demanding trade with the United States and allowing US merchant ships into Japanese ports.

When Yumi explained the many ways to express acceptance in Japan, my understanding of the word was shaped by our friendship.

The next person I asked about the meaning of acceptance was Yuko Enomoto, whom I met about twenty years ago in Tokyo.*

Yuko gave me three words:

ukeireru

jkukugo

jiko jyu yuu

"*Jiko jyu yuu* means 'self-acceptance,'" Yuko said. "We can feel it. *Jkukugo* is perhaps more intellectual, while *ukeireru* is kind of easy to understand and fun to imagine inside oneself."

Of all the people I know in Japan, Yuko is the most urbane. The two of us met through *Slow Food*, the Italian food organization, and she is the person who taught me a great deal about hidden teahouses, coffee salons, art galleries, and

---

*Yuko is a writer and also edited Ted Bestor's epic, classic book about Tsukiji, the world-famous fish market (the book was co-translated by Shinichi Fukuoka and Masako Wanami). Bestor is an eminent Harvard anthropologist whose work is essential reading if you're interested in discovering more about Japan.

tiny neighborhood restaurants in Tokyo. Nowadays, with a husband who is one of the most highly regarded up-and-coming chefs in the city (cooking Italian and Peruvian cuisines) and a toddler son who appears to be the embodiment of goodness, Yuko is striking a balance between her professional gifts and the demands of motherhood, accepting what comes her way with insouciance.

A third person whose help I received was Kiyomi Tsurusawa. I first met Kiyomi ages ago at the Kayotei, my favorite *ryokan* (hot springs inn) in Japan, located in Yamanaka in the prefecture of Ishikawa. She was the interpreter over several days for work we were doing on a book about artisans of the region. We talked about traditional crafts back then, but also a lot about our shared love of jazz.*

"Many Japanese words can be translated as acceptance," said Kiyomi. "It's very tough, but here are six. And oh, we have more!"

shodaku

jyu yuu

shiji

ninjyu

gokaku

ukeireru

"*Shodaku* can mean accepting an invitation. *Jyu yuu* can mean accepting a present. *Shiji* can mean accepting an idea or thought. *Ninjyu* can mean accepting difficulties. *Gokaku*

---

*Kiyomi is a big fan of Miles Davis, especially his recording "Someday My Prince Will Come."

can mean accepting a person. And *ukeireru* can mean accepting reality."

In the end, I fell in love with this definition of *ukeireru*: "Used by a mother with a child to accept something gently, fun to imagine inside oneself, accepting reality."

What would it be like to act each day inspired by *ukeireru*? What might we do? What might we say? What sorts of things can we participate in and advance in order to have that sense of well-being brought about by acceptance?

Ukeireru means much more than *self*-acceptance. It means acceptance of our relationships in our families, in school, at work, and in our communities. It means accepting others. It means accepting reality and creating contexts that broaden the narrow, confining, and exhausting perspective of Self.

Through embracing the ephemeral and imperfect, *ukeireru* applies Zen Buddhist and Shinto principles to modern Japan to create well-being and satisfaction. This is evident in a shared aesthetic approach that started and developed centuries ago. The art established a way of seeing. Originating at the top through a, let's say, collaboration between religious institutions and feudal lords, the aesthetic turned the tables on loss that actually is due to ignorance: few institutions, little science, rigid social-economic structures, a ruthless natural environment. Rather than despair over life's harsh conditions, the aesthetic established that the meaning of life was accepting, embracing, and even seeking loss.

The goal is to create a mental state in which you feel at home with sufficient awareness and confidence. You accept and embrace loss. You also realize that however you define yourself, that realization is contingent upon affiliation with nature and society.

We operate *here* in a society that cherishes the individual and that makes happiness the goal, and if those things come at the expense of others, that's too bad for them too much of the time.

"Win or go home."

"My way or the highway."

"What's in it for me?"

What *ukeireru* does is magnify the relationships in which we find ourselves; it provides the strength needed to make changes that are personal as well as structural.

In order to change anything—big like systemic racism or small like bad customer service—you need to have a calm state of mind and proceed with focus, deliberation, and intensity. You need a plan.

The plan is to accept yourself, your family, your friends, your colleagues, and your community. As you do this, you might be able to understand other points of view.

If you're not self-aware, and you lack a state of calm self-awareness, you won't be able to change things, especially not the conditions that created or contributed to the stress in the first place.

Create well-being, and then, if you like, address the problems that contributed to your isolation, worrying, and sadness. This isn't a call to arms. It's not: hot green tea, a long bath, a nap, and then let's take to the streets. But if you want, you can take the energy that comes from being calm and try to make necessary changes.

Practicing the habits and adopting the behaviors associated with Japanese culture have helped me to observe and read and write with more concentration and comprehension than ever. Time seems to slow down—I'm not always thinking ahead, and I'm not always thinking back. *Ukeireru* creates a kind of basic state of immediacy—of being present.

Seeing and accepting more fully a situation from the point of view of another person, with whom I'm angry and disagree, has enabled me to recognize that a lot of things that used to upset me often don't matter. If I'm upset with someone I love or work with, a friend or a stranger, I'm better able to delay reacting or maybe not react at all. Why should any of it matter? It matters because I give it the power to matter. But it may not matter intrinsically, and for sure in a matter of months, it may not matter at all. By that time, I'll have something new to worry or be miserable about.

Or if it does matter, if it's a real problem that causes stress and needs to be addressed, accepting the situation at the time, and not reacting to it angrily or immediately, grants the time to suss out what might be a solution rather than a *reaction*.

I'm better able to understand that whatever is upsetting probably has more to do with *who's* upsetting me than with me. The person who is aggravating has to live with aggravation regularly. I'm just getting a glimpse of what it's like to be them.

If you think that a person is a real pain, believe me, they are a real pain to themselves. If a person is a jerk in a forest, and no one else is there, is the person still a jerk?

I love the way that the Japanese perspective of things lasting *briefly* can be applied to everyday life.

Recognizing the stress and exhaustion of anger also helps to keep it at bay. Few people feel good after being angry, and the main way to relieve *that* stress is to get angry again. What a colossal distraction, what a waste of time and energy.

With awareness, I do the best I can to steer clear of what's causing stress, which includes not just situations but highly destructive individuals. (You know who you are by my absence.) Instead of all the negativity, I try hard to focus and establish connections to the people and things that sustain me.

Ukeireru does *not* mean subservience, giving in, accepting conditions that are destructive, or surrendering to abusive or exploitative relationships. More than anything, it means understanding that each one of us is defined in large part by those around us; it means not thinking about ourselves as independent of these relationships.

And it means that through letting go of self-centered ideals, we gain traction to change those situations that cause so much pain and can participate in and establish relationships that are loving and respectful.

A chief difference between Japan and the United States in terms of self-identity is that here the individual has more authority than the group. In Japan, it's the reverse: the group establishes your principal identity.

Hayao Kawai, a great Japanese psychologist, gave a superlative example of how the difference plays out. In his book

Buddhism and the Art of Psychotherapy, Dr. Kawai writes that a typical Japanese speaker will apologize before giving a speech, and say, "I have to begin by saying that I am not qualified to be a lecturer here and have no knowledge that allows me to talk about psychotherapy." That's because "when people in Japan gather in one place, they share a feeling of unity, regardless of whether they have known each other before or not. One should not stand alone, separated from others." Dr. Kawai contrasts this group identity with a typical US speaker who will often begin a speech with a joke, "enabling all the people there, by laughing together, to experience oneness."

Gordon Mathews adds to this understanding in his book about Japan, noted earlier, by describing the philosopher Esyun Hamaguchi's concept of the differences between Japanese and Western mentalities: "Hamaguchi coins a new term for the Japanese self, *kanjin*, a person whose identity is located in the linkages between self and others, as opposed to the Western *kojin*, whose identity is located within one's autonomous self."

So which is better? The group cohesion of Japan or the self-driven mentality of the United States?

Neither, really. Who wants to feel the confinement of a group, day in and day out? And who wants to feel the loneliness of being cut off from a group, on your own in the world?

I agree with Dr. Kawai, who trained in California and Switzerland, that we ought to bring out the best in both Japanese and US cultures. "In seeking a postmodern consciousness," he writes, "we can, I think, come to know each other and, to our benefit, find something new."

Reasons exist for Japan's development of a culture of acceptance and silence. Even today, ancient styles, ways of relating, mannerisms, cultural mores, and expectations can be seen in relationships, which differ from how friendships, work, leisure, family, and marriage are experienced in the United States.

The habits came about through sets of circumstances that are unique to Japan. Its geographical position in the world meant that things didn't change much over time. For centuries, the culture was more static and isolated than most.

In the United States, geographical isolation from the places where most Americans originated, except the indigenous and those from bordering nations, meant that the character of people here, while shaped by the history and memories and rules of previous generations, could be new.

An American myth is that you can be anyone in this country. You can change your name, your appearance, and your goals. You don't have to abide by group norms. You don't have to be like your parents. You can be born poor and die rich.

Who Wants to Be a Millionaire?

Among the many reasons that Americans feel so much stress in their lives is the sense of falling short of this fantasy, of thinking that the inability to be the person in the myth is the fault of the individual: Your failure comes about because you didn't try hard enough.

But Raj Chetty, an economist at Harvard and Stanford, showed this isn't so. Raj and his team created the Opportunity

Atlas. This atlas demonstrates that your zip code is a greater determinant of future success than individual factors.

Visit the website www.opportunityatlas.org, and type in a zip code. You'll see income levels and where you grow up are inextricable determinants of financial success in later life. Sure, some people emerge with greater success than others in their poor neighborhood, and sure, some kids growing up in rich neighborhoods become poor. But most people, according to the data, stay put.

So much for the American Dream of individual hard work leading to success. The message isn't: don't work hard. The message is: if at first you don't succeed, it might be due to systemic lack of economic opportunities based on race, gender, and class.

Understanding your stress isn't *just* yours alone broadens the discussion. It means that you are part of larger groups, rich or poor, black or white or Asian or Hispanic, middle class or blue collar, straight or LGBTQ, young or old, and that what makes you unhappy probably makes others in your group, or several groups of which you are a part, unhappy, too. You are not alone.

It helps to know that the stress you're experiencing isn't just personal. Whatever steps you take toward self-improvement are good, but in addition to these, the sources of stress in your group won't go away until they're addressed.

Learn to live with systemic causes of stress or not—that's your choice. Either way, it's nice to know *why* you might be scared and miserable.

Any book about happiness gains more legitimacy by making note of the economics of *un*happiness.

As Raj said to me, "I have family around the world. And I know that achievement is not merely the result of hard work."*

While myths can be inspiring and can in part define a narrative for many citizens of the same country, they also create burdens and stress when taken literally.

It's really not true that you can be anyone you like in the United States, or that you will make so much money that you surpass the economic class you were born into, or that you can treat the world as if you're a sheriff or gold prospector in the Wild West. Sure, many people here do, in fact, transcend their origins and do amass fortunes, but academic studies demonstrate that where they were born and the circumstances in which they were raised are pretty much where *most* people are going to stay.

The winners hit the lottery or jackpot, but that's hardly the same or similar to the myth of the American Dream.

The playwright David Mamet said in an interview that the reason why movie studios pay him such exorbitant sums for his scripts is to dazzle and distract just about everyone else. By having a few winners, the "losers" can hold on to unrealistic dreams of making it big rather than changing the system. It's like living inside a casino.

---

*My interview with Raj appears in my book *Those Immigrants! Indians in America: A Psychological Exploration of Achievement* (New Delhi: Fingerprint, 2016).

It's exciting to imagine that the myths are inspiring, and that's great, but it also means that the institutions—schools, banks, employers, law enforcement agencies, medical systems, courts—that restrict movement aren't seen as problematic as they are in reality.

So then it's possible to tell yourself some awful things: It's your fault you're not happy. Your fault that you never achieved your dreams.

Myths are there to distract people from making changes that will replace them. And they are brutally punishing, ripe for self-loathing.

Belief in myths stymies action that could deal with the sources of stress realistically.

If you convince yourself you can be anyone in America, and you don't achieve that goal, who's to blame?

You are.

As if.

Japan's myths are also specific to its development as a nation. One defining myth is that of surface cohesion: things must look prim and proper, and the group must participate in creating that appearance.*

---

*Japanese schools require *o-soji*, a cleaning up of classrooms and corridors. Western media report this event like it's some amazing act of self-sacrifice and pride. The schools are spotless, but there are *few inclusive* special education programs and not many classroom modifications for children with learning disabilities. Progress is assessed by taking countless standardized exams rather than participating in discussions or analyzing written works.

The push toward surface cohesion in Japan may have come about because it was key long ago to survival. Faced with dangers of nature and isolation, the individual didn't stand a chance. And rice farming, the centuries-old centerpiece of Japan's economy, requires large numbers of people laboring in groups. Surface cohesion is meant to be inspiring and a way to be safe and productive: work together with others to create the *appearance* of a harmonious group norm.

On a positive note, this means: Think of the effect of your behavior on others before you act. Don't disrupt the flow. If we don't act together, we may not be doing our best.

The country has harsh, forbidding geography, and few other places on earth have to deal with as many earthquakes, tsunami, and volcanic eruptions.

On top of periodic catastrophes and crises even today, Japan's mountainous, sea level, and industrialized landscapes mean that, according to the *CIA World Factbook*, only 11.7 percent of its land is arable, which ranks it fifty-first in the world, behind Cameroon, Sudan, Pakistan, Italy, and so on. As a result, famines, subsistence diets, and sharecropping defined its agriculture until about seventy years ago.

With newfound wealth, Japan gets a lot of food products from abroad. Rice from Southeast Asia, fruit from South America and Africa, and soybeans from the United States and China. Most of the soy sauce, tofu, and miso celebrated in Japanese products are made from soybeans grown outside of the country.

Topography and food supplies are a big part of what defines a nation, and added to this is Japan's geographical isolation from the mainland. The foreign influences that shape Japanese culture—Chinese, Korean, Portuguese, Dutch, American, and now the whole world—arrived and fermented and grew and were shaped, in turn, by the isolated society already there.

All this contributed to placing the *Japanese* group at the center of consciousness and social cohesion. A great way to create groups is to build shared experiences, chiefly visual and repetitive, that everyone does in the same way.

The task is to preserve and promote individual differences in ways that are respectful. Comparable, in reverse, to the American tendency to blame oneself for not achieving the American Dream, in Japan there is a tendency to blame oneself for not fitting in with or conforming to group norms and expectations.

And yet, just as our highly individualistic culture has great benefits, so, too, does Japan's excellence at establishing groups.

How you are expected to act in a public bath. Prayers. Daily ways of eating and drinking. Displays of respect. Above all: silent *acceptance* of the other person and your surroundings.

Japanese culture synthesized individual behaviors with social structures in highly original ways. The synthesis, which included the development of group consciousness and belonging over individualism, made acceptance or *ukeireru* essential to survival.

Although Japan is both celebrated and belittled for being a nation that refines rather than invents or creates, it is also a nation where originality in the arts has always been possible.

Famous for refinement, Japan is also a deeply original nation.

Although the group matters in Japan more than in most places, individual efforts—*if they benefit the group through original approaches that avoid conflict or show dimensions that were not understood before*—are valued. Striving for perfection is part of everyday life in Japan, and while falling short is natural, having goals that reinforce the community, whether it is bullet trains or safe cities or accessible, affordable medical care, are part of what life is about there.

Then, too, it is through the art and gastronomy of Japan that creation of shared pleasures add to group culture and well-being.

The traditional range of what's seen and eaten and how it is eaten is narrow, meaning that people do not diverge much from one another. The limited variety can deepen the experience. Since *yakitori* or *ramen* or *udon* or *soba* or *gohan* or *tonkatsu* is what's served typically throughout many establishments, Japanese are often eating the same foods. And restaurants often serve only one ingredient, or they serve set menus and everyone eats the same things. Many restaurants do not have menus: the chef decides (*omakase*) what everyone will eat.*

It makes me think of Thanksgiving: knowing that across the United States most of us are eating turkey means to me

---

*Which can raise challenges for Western visitors with food allergies or preferences.

that the shared experience has the potential to have us all feel and think similarly—at least for one day.

That sometimes happens, naturally, when everyone eats the same thing in the same way—from where chopsticks are placed on the table to when rice is supposed to be eaten to where and how you should sit.

It's like the line from "We the People" by A Tribe Called Quest sung by Q-Tip: "When we get hungry, we eat the same fucking food, the ramen noodle."

In Japan, that sameness takes place daily and nationally. Eating the same food is a sign to others that you have something in common with them.

It's being part of a group when eating and also an effort to be part of nature from what's on the plate. Nature as a facet of group experience is a contemporary experience.

It started a long time ago.

During the Heian period (794–1185), nature emerged prominently as a subject in Japanese art. What caught the attention of artists back then, which continues to influence awareness, is a form of *ukeireru*, evident in the focus on things that don't last long: cherry blossoms, frogs, crickets, fireflies, and so on.

The novelist Haruki Murakami writes about this attachment to and acceptance of brevity and how he prizes things that are quick to disappear. If we don't pay attention, if we do not observe as fully as we can, we are lost; we are cut off from nature.

Murakami wrote: "Cherry blossoms, fireflies and red leaves lose their beauty within a very short time. . . . And we are somewhat relieved to confirm that they are not merely beautiful but already beginning to fall, to lose their small lights and their vivid beauty. We find peace of mind in the fact that the peak of beauty has passed and disappeared."

After the thing is gone, we can embrace its absence. The absence is as important as the presence. Maybe more important. Peace of mind *from* loss. That's a profound form of acceptance.

The Muromachi period (1336–1573) followed, and so did *yugen. Yu* has been explained to me by Japanese as something that is *unfathomable* or *mysterious.* The term or concept is fundamental to the art and psychology of Japan: things are implied; indirectness is a way to invite greater observation. That increased observation makes demands: you have to be silent; you have to listen, to absorb, and to believe that what you see and experience may be a representation of some other hidden core that you will only glimpse or reach through setting yourself and your opinions aside. Through this process, you join others who are also trying to figure things out. And you become part of the thing observed in an effort to try to understand it. Beauty as implied rather than directly experienced, an approach that is not understood unless you are quietly observing, appreciating its temporality, accepting that there is both more *and* less than what's happening.

When we come face-to-face with something that has elements of *yugen*, we can wind up being in that thing, being part of what's happening rather than separated from it. Because to understand, appreciate, and accept the observation, you have to concentrate long and hard and silently. You can't allow your biases and perspectives to guide you; if you do, you will miss the thing itself, and you won't understand its meaning independent of you.

When you look at Japanese calligraphy, porcelain, lacquerware, or *washi* (paper), you can acquire a sense of being part of the object—not only through observing the art but in knowing that others are probably sharing the same or very similar observations. The uniformity of the aesthetic, how it is created to evoke responses shared by many, is part of creating a group mentality in Japan.

The Japanese term *nihon no kokoro*, which might be thought of as meaning the heart of Japan, is one way to express these phenomena of aesthetic union.[*]

By accepting our place in the scheme of things, we are better able to think and feel with focus and deep concentration. More observation and less opinion means more acceptance.

Develop insight as well as an ability to observe, and through both try to understand what nature expects of you and what is truest about yourself. By doing that, it's possible

---

[*]Donald Keene, who lived in Tokyo most of his life and whose wonderful writing made millions around the world more aware of Japan, describes the aesthetic experience as epitomized by being "in a typical Japanese room with *tatami* covering the floor, *shoji*, a *tokonoma* containing an ink painting and a flower arrangement, and, just outside, an unobtrusive garden that is an essential part of the room."

to accept how others might feel, think, fear, and desire, and how you might be of help to them. You may also have the requisite energy to change or address the sources of stress in your life.

(Hint: It's not about you. It's about you in relationship to others and your surroundings.)

Through insight into your imperfections and awareness of the brevity of life, *ukeireru* compels you to slow down and absorb what and who are around you. Life isn't perfect, no relationship is perfect, and you had better appreciate the present because it's all over very quickly. (No pain lasts forever.)

A famous poem by Ezra Pound, who was influenced by the haiku tradition of poetry in Japan, is a good example of what *ukeireru* means:

> *And the days are not full enough*
> *And the nights are not full enough*
> *And life slips by like a field mouse*
> *Not shaking the grass*

Live life fully, close to nature, accepting that time is short and that no matter what we do, nature is not moved or shaken by our frailty and actions. We are insignificant.

There are *practical ways* in which *ukeireru* can be applied to our lives. These are activities that get us away from self-preoccupation. Recognizing that one's happiness ultimately matters less than how others are feeling. Understanding that our well-being depends on the satisfaction

we give people. Taking time out from each day to participate in nonproductive experiences that help us escape from
ourselves and enable us to feel refreshed or rejuvenated
afterward.

This way of thinking and social organization is centuries
old in Japan. What other nation has a classic book about
the merits of doing nothing? Called *Essays in Idleness* and
written between 1330 and 1332 by the Zen Buddhist monk
Yoshida Kenkō, this book celebrates the value of observing
and the calm that comes from letting go of one's personal
concerns.

These efforts to establish acceptance of where we stand in
relationship to nature and people then provide a calm state
that can be useful in changing how we got stressed out in the
first place.

When Jerry Seinfeld tells Judd Apatow, in his interview
about the meaning of comedy, that he keeps a map of the
galaxy in his office to remember his insignificance in order
to take the pressure off, that's *ukeireru*. (Seinfeld added: "I'm
drawn to a lot of Zen stuff.") In a later interview with Howard Stern, Seinfeld adds to his observation: "I'm not big on
enjoyment. I don't think it's important. I think what's important is *they* [the audience] enjoy it."

When Ariana Huffington starts a company that provides
space for people to take naps during the workday, that's
ukeireru. *Close your eyes*—don't be productive.

When *Afar* magazine reports that urban centers where
people bathe together are showing up in major cities, that's
ukeireru.

In Japan, you experience *ukeireru* in the coffee salons, rooms for naps, public celebrations of small and seasonal changes, and communal baths. Throughout the day, and all over the country, from work to home, Japanese men and women try hard to keep calm, pay attention to the needs of others, and accept their place in the natural scheme of things.

To the extent that harmony and community are evident in Japan, and contribute to well-being, it is through *ukeireru* being applied successfully to everyday life.

A Zen koan or parable I think about a lot illustrates the power of *ukeireru*: The Buddha comes to a village and is immediately surrounded by worshipful people who sing his praises. But one man stands apart from the crowd and denounces the Buddha angrily. He rants for a long time, saying that the Buddha is a thief, that he only wants riches and fame. Finally, the Buddha asks him if he is done yelling, and when the man says that he is, the Buddha asks him, "If you give someone a gift and the person refuses to take it, whom does the gift belong to?" The man sneers and laughs and says that this is typical of the Buddha's stupidity. "It belongs to the person who offered the gift," he says. "Any fool knows that!" The Buddha says, "Exactly. And your anger is your gift. I refuse to accept it. It therefore belongs to you. No one wants your anger."

This is how *ukeireru* works. Imagine coming up with routine ways of dealing with anger, fear, and arguments that are unlike what you've tried up to now. Not reacting, but taking in the situation, understanding and accepting what the other person feels, and then deciding to take a course of action (or inaction) that reframes things within a context of the relationship.

I think about that koan when I get an angry email or meet someone rude or am spoken to disrespectfully, and remember that the anger belongs to the other person.[*]

Through an awareness of the importance of groups, Japan has a cohesive, pragmatic society: no mass shootings, no opiate epidemic, great urban safety, public decorum, and the proportion of women working in Japan is higher than in the United States.[†]

---

[*] Caution: Japan's problems are related to its *over-reliance* on groups for adding meaning to individual lives. People can feel ashamed of being sad—they might blame themselves because they feel as if they are letting the group down by "indulging" in an emotion that causes others pain. Psychotherapy and counseling hardly exist. There is pressure to be part of the group even when one's individual identity is unhinged by giving in to group think.

[†] Only since 2011, and, yes, usually not in high-paying jobs or leadership positions, and at the cost of having to choose between a career and having children, and often in contractual, one- or two-year positions. Some companies are even requiring women employees in administrative positions to wear high heels and, if they need eyeglasses, to wear contact lenses instead. No one would look to Japan for leadership on women's rights. Women are not part of the core pinnacles in Japan, and that exclusionary practice by the top groups keeps them from having the authority needed to make change. Japanese men have the willingness and desire to be unyielding, lacking in insight and fairness, in common with other men on the planet.

Japanese also live longer on average compared to people in the United States and spend less on health care. The Japanese budget allocates 10.2 percent to health care, while here it is 17 percent—with better outcomes in Japan.

Part of the success of Japanese well-being is owed to the willingness to benefit groups (over individual rights) with public health measures.

Acceptance, Longevity, and Community

The United States is thirty-fifth globally in life expectancy; Japan is second.* Or, as David Pilling writes in his book *The Growth Delusion*, "The Japanese spend half as much and live four years longer than Americans."†

Life expectancy in the United States has fallen three years in a row; according to CDC data, "this troubling trend is largely driven by deaths from drug overdose and suicide. Life expectancy gives us a snapshot of the nation's overall health and these sobering statistics are a wakeup call that we are losing too many Americans, too early and too often, to conditions that are preventable."

Acceptance also has bearing upon how societies address inequalities, entitlement, and baseline support for those who are most vulnerable, don't have roles to play in a skill-based economy, have chronic physical and mental disorders, lack adequate education, or simply don't fit in. Rather than

---

*Hong Kong is first with overall (male and female) longevity at 84.7. Japanese longevity is 84.5. The U.S. is at 78.9.
† Now it is about six years longer.

marginalize these individuals or segregate or stigmatize or try to deport them, it would be better to implement rules and standards that accept their value as human beings. Japan falls short, but less short than the rest of the world on these integrative measures *for Japanese.*[*]

Ukeireru contributes to Japanese living longer and more comfortably than anywhere else on earth. It is *not* the *cause*; it *is* a major contributing factor. Affluence, community, and tradition in Japan benefit from *ukeireru.*

By combining *our* openness, diversity, and emotional flexibility here with *ukeireru*, we have, as Dr. Kawai noted, the remarkable chance to create a new model of a satisfying, long life and well-being.

It is not primarily about individual gain or self-improvement. Greater significance is achieved by creating

---

*According to the Organization for Economic Cooperation and Development (OECD) in 2015, the ratio of the average income of the richest 10 percent to the poorest 10 percent in Japan is 4.5 percent, compared to 18.5 percent in the United States.

A recent BBC article noted about Japan: "Not only does the island nation rank highest in Asia by the World Bank for overall government effectiveness, rule of law and political stability, it also received the highest marks in Asia from the Social Progress Index for its access to basic knowledge, water and sanitation, and access to nutrition and medical care.

"Health insurance is universal, though it can be expensive since it's income-based and taken out of wages—but residents can go to any doctor any time and costs are capped.

"The education system is another of the country's strengths; elementary and secondary school is mandatory, and Japanese schools rank well globally. Though the schools are highly regimented and systematic—which can lead to over-standardization—they have prioritized nutrition as a key part of education, with school lunches prepared with locally grown ingredients and paired with lessons on healthy eating and food history."

and maintaining a sense of well-being through accepting, listening, relating, and valuing community and relationships.

Most important of all: *be of use to others.*

The two cultures of Japan and the United States put together have the potential to be greater than either one. This book is about the modern habits and activities of Japanese that create a powerful and reassuring sense of *ukeireru* to add to what we have here.

And now a few words about cherry-picking, resignation, and cultural appropriation.

Cherry-Picking, Resignation, and Cultural Appropriation

In 1871, three years after formal establishment of the Meiji Restoration, which ended feudalism and restored the emperor, Japanese realized that they needed to catch up with the West if they were to compete in the modern world and avoid being colonized. Toward that end, a delegation called the Iwakura Embassy traveled to the United States and Europe to cherry-pick the best things in each country that Japan might learn from and develop in order to be a stronger nation.

Put simply, public infrastructure like transportation from the United States, parliamentary democracy with a monarch from England, and scientific research methodology and universities from Prussia all had enormous appeal.

Adapting these ways of organizing society to traditional Japanese ways led to hybrid forms of doing things and served to modernize Japan and turn it into a great world power.

So it's fair to say that this book, inspired by the Iwakura delegation, is cherry-picking. The Japanese delegation picked what they believed to be the best things about the West. We can pick what we believe are the best things about Japan.

Just as the individualism of the West is cause for celebration, so the harmony of being in a group in Japan is essential to well-being. We can learn from one another by accepting what's best about our societies.

Let's not repeat the mistakes.

Which brings me to resignation. There's either a big difference between acceptance and resignation or a thin line. Depends on what you mean and who you are.

I think there *is* a big difference, and here's what I mean: If a situation or relationship requires patience and observation, accept it for the time being. Be strategic rather than tactical. The situation may change. Whether it changes or stays the same may have nothing to do with what you do or say at the moment. If you react to it from a personal perspective, you may find that you have made things worse. You may be literally outgunned.

It may not be fair, that's true, but what can you do to change it so that it doesn't happen again? Think long-term: plan and organize and build a group consensus. For sure, it's probably not happening just to you. It might be systemic or institutional or driven by a screwy relationship. And since it may not be just about you, you have a good chance of getting others to work with you to change things that are unjust. You are not alone.

Resignation, on the other hand, is a gnawing passivity. An insecurity about who you are and what you can do. Theft of authority. An uncertainty about yourself. Recognition that you are denied rights to which you are entitled as a human being. Theft of identity leads to anger, which is a poor substitute for emotion.

The Japanese express resignation with this phrase: *shikata ga nai*. It translates roughly to "It can't be helped" or "Nothing can be done about it." Even when a situation can perhaps change through the action of those in it, the fallback position is *shikata ga nai*.

The phrase *shikata ga nai* reflected a dangerous fatalism and passivity on the part of many Japanese who had been educated to accept the inevitable and neither argue with authority nor fight against arbitrary and bureaucratic rules. This statement of resignation was made by ordinary Japanese living under military rule.

Or as John Hersey wrote in his classic book *Hiroshima*, to explain why victims of the atomic bombing no longer received medical care: it can't be helped; it is pointless; *shikata ga nai*.

Resignation is dangerous. Maybe something *can* be done; maybe something *ought* to be done; maybe action *is* needed. Resignation can also become characteristic of a person, who then becomes passive in other situations.

This book is not about *shikata ga nai*. It's not about giving up or giving in.

On the contrary: if you can acquire self-acceptance, and then acceptance of others and your place in the natural scheme of things, you can recognize your responsibility for thinking of others before you act. As a result, you are more likely to take action that benefits the world you live in: Why choose to make things worse when you feel affiliation for those in your community?

Finally, cultural appropriation needs to be addressed. I'm not Japanese, I don't pretend to be, and you shouldn't either (unless, of course, you are). Just as Japanese modernized by cherry-picking what they believed to be the best of the West, and adapted those things to their culture, you can cherry-pick what you love about Japan.

I'm not suggesting you wear a kimono or take up flower arranging—though if that turns out to be your thing, do it with respect and a recognition that you are showing tribute to and honoring another culture you are irrevocably separated from. Don't be an imposter. Don't pretend to be someone you're not. Don't take something that doesn't belong to you and rob it of its true meaning.

Independent of cultural appropriation, accept yourself for who you are before trying to become who you want to be and might be capable of being.

It's like Michelle Obama wrote in her memoir, *Becoming*: "It was possible, I knew, to live on two planes at once—to have one's feet planted in reality, but pointed in the direction of progress. . . . You got somewhere by building that better reality, if only in your own mind. . . . You may live in the world as it is, but you can still work to create the world as it should be."

Chapter
Three

Breathing in Harmony

Who we are, and *what we can become,* is defined by our relationships to one another. In Japan, those relationships begin and develop through a vast array of shared activities in which the individualism of the participants is defined and understood through their participation. The activity of the group becomes the focal point.

These activities bring people closer to one another, their families, and their communities. Through participation, individual well-being increases as well; ironically, by having the opportunity to forget yourself for a while, you might feel better about yourself. Less of a preoccupation with yourself implies a concern for others and a greater interest in and capacity for observation and acceptance.

The tea ceremony is a ponderous, lengthy, highly ritualized activity that is worth participating in. A well-known white North American cultural anthropologist and scholar of Japan rolled his eyes and stroked his beard and patted his belly when I told him that I enjoyed the ceremony.

"Once," he said, "is enough."

What he meant, as I shared in his subsequent laughter, is that the rather detailed, focused, repetitive, and s-l-o-w nature of the tea ceremony is for most people, here and in Japan, something out of the ordinary. Where one sits, how one sits, the phrases that must be said and when said, the tone, the weightiness of it all—well, it requires a kind of patience that is more often associated with fulfillment of a deeper fantasy than a hot cup of tea.

But what is important, the takeaway, is the connection to a country through a beverage. Germany has Oktoberfest; Japan has its tea ceremony.

Equally important is the recognition that the frailty of the tea ceremony, in contrast to its regimentation, can be applied to numerous other experiences. When participating, I step back and push the world away. Then, on later occasions, in line at the supermarket with a fussy person ahead of me, stuck in traffic, having to deal with a disrespectful individual in a park who doesn't know me, I can take the meditation and quiet inculcated from the whisking of the tea, and wait. Few things are as important as they seem; it's like Drake said, "Had a moment but it came and went."

The tea ceremony is the epitome, the height of a cultural experience, and what informs it, how it is structured, and how you feel when doing it can all be helpful in navigating far less structured situations and relationships: sit still; pay attention; follow rules; go slowly; enjoy a simple experience.

The silence and observation of everyday life, as simple as having coffee or tea or even cocktails, are very much part of what Japanese call *aun no kokyu*. As the writer and editor Yoji Yamakuse puts it in his wonderful book *Japaneseness*, this means "breathing in harmony." He explains, "If you understand the position of the person you are dealing with, and you are able to properly play your role, then you will be able to control the flow of conversation in that particular setting, and it will not be necessary for you to use many words to do so."

The Japanese tea ceremony is well known. Most people don't engage routinely at home in the use of the various cleaning cloths or ladle, the whisking of the powdery tea, the slow pouring, the repetitive bows, and the downright finicky way of pouring and holding the cup, turning it this way and that laboriously—all of which are necessary parts of the ritual. However, people are still informed by the slowness and meditation of the tea ceremony when they enjoy a cup of ordinary green tea in Japan.

In Japanese *ryokan*, each room typically has a tall thermos plugged in and filled with hot water. Next to this, on a small and round lacquer tray, is a tiny pot, a strainer, and a little canister that holds fresh, aromatic green tea.

Before or after a nap, before or after a soak in the hot springs, in your *yukata* (a thin cotton robe), you make a pot of tea, and wait a bit while it steeps.

The tea cups in Japan are small enough to fit into the palm of an average adult's hand. At a *ryokan*, you sit on the *tatami* mat of the room, lounge back, and sip tea, feeling dreamy and, as you try to stay awake, thinking perhaps of Bashō, the great poet who wrote this in the seventeenth century:

A monk sips morning tea,
it's quiet,
the chrysanthemum's flowering.

You can do this at home and at work. Not the ritual, but the tea itself. You need: good green tea leaves, a teapot, a strainer, hot water nearly boiling.

Throughout each day, employees drink numerous cups of green tea. This has the effect of punching a hole in the schema of relentless productivity, creating a shared activity with coworkers, and sparking memories of times spent drinking tea in bucolic settings. Then, too, the tea can readily conjure up images of the gorgeous terraces of tea plants.

The experience is more than the tea itself, but it is also about the tea. The tea has a fresh aroma that can coax your olfactory senses into a kind of rapturous state as you picture or even feel nature in a cup. And more than the tea, it is nature, past and present, enjoyed either individually or with another person who is having tea with you, that can bring about a sense of well-being, a forgetting of who you are and where you are, while at the same time reinforcing your grasp of the pleasure of feeling safe and alive.

I think of Bashō's monk sipping tea and accepting the quiet of morning that brought him to a place where his observation of a flowering plant took precedence in his consciousness. No, not every cup is going to send you hurtling back in time or create inner peace. Note that Bashō's protagonist is a monk. Are you a monk? I didn't think so. But if you add green tea to your daily activities, especially if you are sharing a cup with a loved one or friend or colleague, you might find time slowing down. You might observe more, you might accept the people you are with more fully, *and* you might enjoy the slight caffeine buzz.*

Some of the best green tea comes from Shizuoka prefecture, a region of Japan with terraced plots of low tea plants that are beautiful in the rain and before a harvest. When I visited, as we drove along the steep hillsides, the perfect rows of tea plants, each identical in height and color, suggested to me the possibility of order and plentitude, of hard work, and of dedication against the odds.

Tea production in Shizuoka is threatened by many factors, including competition from China (where salaries are much lower); a younger generation, as is true around the world, that is leaving the countryside for more economic and social opportunities in cities; and the massive production costs of tea farming.†

---

*The amount of caffeine in green tea varies, depending on the brand and brewing time. In the United States, most brands are pretty low in caffeine, while in Japan tea has about four times the amount found here. I can attest to that: in Japan, during the course of a day of meetings, each of which has green tea served that all of us are expected to drink, I am often alert long past my usual bedtime. Drink, as always, in moderation.

† An article in nippon.com notes that in Japan, "According to the 2015 census, the average age of people primarily engaged in agriculture has increased by 7.2 years over the last decade to 67. . . . The increasing age of farmers and subsequent decrease in labor input is considered a key factor in the growing number of fallow and abandoned agricultural fields around the country, raising concerns about farming areas going to ruin." How can tea survive? Subsidies. Agriculture is heavily subsidized by the Japanese government, and while much of this goes to the politically

So you can enjoy a product that is a synecdoche of Japan as well as support farming communities that need your help.

In the United States, green tea is available all over, from convenience stores inside gas stations to supermarkets, but if you want one of the best, try Ippodo. This centuries-old tea shop, based in Kyoto, opened a satellite store in the Murray Hill section of Manhattan, and if you don't live in New York (I don't), you can order the tea online and have it delivered to you by mail from Japan. The online shop has a big selection of their teas, including organic and caffeine-free, as well as suggestions for ways to pair the tea with sweet or savory dishes.

A Cup of Coffee, Please

Japan is also the third largest consumer of coffee in the world (after the United States and Germany). Coffee salons occupied an important place in the previous political culture and still do in the current life of Japanese.

A regimented society, like others with histories of a ruling class, Japan had little mingling in public places before Westernization. *Here* was where aristocrats went, *here* is where the monks went, *here* is where the men went, and *here* are the demimonde, traders, and poor neighborhoods. The country

---

important rice farmers, who support the ruling party, tea depends on government money in order to survive. Nokyo, the Central Union of Agricultural Co-Operatives, which includes the tea farmers, is continually fighting imports of competing products into Japan, seeking more tax breaks from the government, and prioritizing their demands for subsidies. That's a precarious future.

was segmented, and coffee salons went a long way to breaking down barriers.

Coffee came from Brazil, where Japanese went in the nineteenth century as indentured farmers on plantations before later becoming organizers and merchants and exporters. The early salons were among the first public spaces where Japanese men and women from a range of economic classes could sit and relax without strictures. Adding to the coalescence was jazz.

Jazz is still a big part of the coffee culture in Japan, and upon entering my first salon, in Tokyo, hearing Bud Powell on the perfect sound system, followed by John Coltrane, Miles Davis, and Ben Webster, all I felt was: wow. It suggested immediately that what I thought I knew about Japan was way off base.

As Kenny Garrett told me, "About the audiences who come to hear jazz, I'll say this: In general, Japanese culture is about conformity, but it's also about people seeking to become individuals. The great drummer and bandleader Art Blakey exposed Japanese to music that is about that."

Jazz remains a big part of that exploration and experience: the freedom, even the encouragement to let go, to improvise, to make all of that acceptable public behavior. It's allowed to be an individual; the group gives you permission!

The first coffee salons were places where people from varying backgrounds could talk freely, batting around ideas that were often Western in origin. The radicalism of that was so threatening back in the day that salons were shut down by police when Japan became a totalitarian dictatorship.

Nowadays, the salons are everywhere and even though international franchises threaten their existence, they hold a special place in the hearts of Japanese. And that's in part because of the way the coffee is served.

You start by picking out the freshly roasted beans (often in containers with signs indicating when roasting took place) with guidance from the barista. If you are a regular, the barista knows what you want before you ask. Or, better yet, you can let the barista decide for you. Then the beans are placed in a tiny grinder and ground up by hand. The barista heats the water to a temperature that he or she deems perfect (or that the barista remembers you preferred from your recent visit) and then slowly pours it over the ground beans, which are held in either a pour-over coffee brewer, or through a narrow drip sieve. We're talking ballpark ten to fifteen minutes in silence except for the grind, the water heating, the slow pour, and the old school jazz.

Whether the result is better than a more, let's say, efficient approach is for others to decide. What I know is that the visuals and slow pace are definitely part of the experience. It's relaxing to take time out from the day. To remove yourself from the fast pace imposed on you.

It's wonderful to surrender to the expert behind the counter, to allow him or her to decide which beans are best, which roast is best, which grind is best, how long to boil the water, and how and when to drink the coffee. Oh, sure, you can choose, but why bother? The barista is the coffee master, the teacher, the person to whom you are granting *omakase*—the right to decide. This sets the tempo, the mood, and while the coffee had better be good—it's usually great—what matters is that you are acting as if you are in the barista's home. This surrender is a way to show trust and invite intimacy.

Throughout US cities there are increasing numbers of Japanese coffee salons, and once you enter the world created by them, chances are you will gain a sense of well-being. It is wondrous to manipulate time by way of both the slow preparation of coffee and the swift rush coming from the caffeine. All this accompanied by saxophone and piano and trumpet and drums and bass from recordings made over sixty years ago. What's cool, too, is how the experience of the coffee mirrors the music: the slowing down in both is the objective structure, while the improvisation derives from the personal experience.

At home, you can recreate this.

I bought a terrific Japanese hand grinder, and at night—not every night—I slowly grind the beans for the next morning. You can get yourself a Japanese glass vessel that brews the coffee, too, and stand back and pour until you have the desired cup. Even if you don't indulge in this laborious process, it's still possible to take it slow by sipping and mulling and doing the best you can to savor the taste rather than wait for that exquisite caffeine rush. I mean, you don't drink wine just to get buzzed, right? Show coffee the same respect. Slowing things down means creating the space needed for observation. With observation, you have the opportunity to accept where you are and who you are—less reminiscing, less anxiety about the future, being more present with the simple taste of roasted beans come to life in boiled water. Waiting to enjoy the coffee becomes part of the experience before drinking it.

You Walk into a Bar

Then, too, cocktails. Like so much in Japan that is informed by the West, cocktails are the same as what you find in the United States—and yet completely different. The idea initially was to accept Western customs but adapt them to the Japanese way of doing things. These days enjoying cocktails in Japan is about creating an atmosphere that isn't limited to the individual. The setting and the way drinks are made lead to a group experience.

The idea of drinking cocktails *before* dinner in Japan has not been popular—until lately—because alcohol numbs the senses.* If you are interfering with taste, smell, and vision, the food won't be as good, and it's also an insult to the chef.

What's left? A deep appreciation for seasonality and performance, which can be applied in the United States.

Japanese cocktails make use of fresh herbs, plants, and fruits in season and have as much to do with these ingredients as they do with alcohol. Which means you are tuning

---

*The typical pour in a Japanese bar is one ounce of alcohol. Compare that to the two- or three-ounce pours in US establishments. Lots of reasons for that, including difficulty among about half of all Japanese in breaking down or metabolizing alcohol because of a lack of sufficient amounts of the enzyme aldehyde dehydrogenase. The result can be a flushed face, nausea, fatigue, and rapid drunkenness.

into nature even as you sit in a dark bar in Ginza listening to jazz and slowing things down.

The vessel in which your drink is served also has significance. From the Baccarat crystal in an upscale bar that is used for a whisky cocktail to the tall, slender glass of some concoction with *yuzu*, which is a type of citrus, what you see is as important as what you drink. It's part of the Japanese aesthetic.

Huge blocks of ice from which chunks are broken off with ice picks or shaped into perfect cubes or balls. The bartenders' outfits, cinematic with tuxedos or flat-out goofy with kilts and head scarves, add up to creating an experience or context for the drinks.

So much of what takes place is part of a longer Japanese tradition of the enormous gulf between public and private behavior. The Japanese term for the public self is *tatemae*. The real person was at home. The Japanese term for the private self is *honne*.

People can invent themselves in public, play a role, and act a part so different from who they are in private. It makes for a new reality, and one that is forced on the guests. Bonus: Now you, as a guest, can play a part, too.

Karaoke draws upon this theatrical approach to relationships, and in karaoke parlors in Shinjuku or Shibuya, for example, you can be a cowboy, a rock star, a gangster, you name it. Drinks fuel the show.

This took place for the first time on my first visit nearly twenty years ago on a trip to Park Hyatt to celebrate the opening of *Lost in Translation*. Chefs Daniel Boulud,

Andrew Carmellini, Mark Fiorentino, and Richie Torrissi were the reason for the invitation; Daniel asked me to tag along.* We piled into a Harley-Davidson motorcycle roadhouse karaoke room. Drinks were served. Daniel crooned, "I Did It My Way," Mark jumped on the piano and belted out, "Born to Run," and I growled through "White Riot."

Going to an old school joint, like Bar Lupin in Ginza, which long ago was a hangout for famous Japanese writers like Yasunari Kawabata and Osamu Dazai, provides a different version of this type of experience. The bar is hidden in an alley and down a flight of narrow steps, and while you definitely won't sing there, you'll have a taste of what it is like to be someone else than who you are in private.

The bartender knows this and encourages the show. In fact, as here in the States, the guests are the entertainment. You are watching them; the person tending bar is watching you.

The drinks: the bartender will extend their arms, dazzle with deft wrist action, and, like a magician performing a trick, pour the ice and liquid into a shaker. Then, extending both arms, they shake it madly for nearly a minute. Or stir it methodically with a long metal rod.

---

*Chef Boulud was invited to participate in a junket to Japan through a complicated association of sponsors, from the James Beard Foundation to Park Hyatt to JAL (Japan Airlines). Because I was doing a lot of public radio reporting at the time, Daniel invited me along. I had two weeks' notice to pack my bags. Two other writers, Adam Sachs and Adam Rappaport, joined us, and our entourage explored Tokyo top to bottom. The restaurant crew had to work most of the time, but the other writers and my radio producer were free to do as we liked.

Gen Yamamoto is the biggest star of the current Tokyo bar scene. Lean, tall, and dressed in a white jacket and dark tie, Gen has a tiny eponymous bar in the Azabu-Juban section of town. He focuses here on seasonality in his drinks and serves four to six small, precise drinks per guest and per visit. Time halts in his place, and conversations between strangers take place because we are all having the same cocktails and each one is a harbinger.

"My *kodawari* is *ichigo-ichiei*," Gen told me. *Kodawari* translates roughly to a striving for unreachable perfection achieved through relentless practice, repetition, and extreme attention to detail. *Ichigo-ichiei* means "one chance, one opportunity," and the idea behind it is to recognize, understand, and accept life's brevity. "I am always striving to do my best each time. Otherwise, we can figure it out together."

Each time I go to Gen's place I've had something different. The first time I walked into his place, organized like a sanctum, I had thought of ordering a gin martini. It was that long ago, and I was that wrongheaded and naive. The deal, however, is *omakase* on full throttle. Gen decides, and he's always right.

How could it be otherwise? He spends a ridiculous amount of time researching herbs and plants, finding faraway sources, and then hours and hours and hours trying to perfect his drinks so that they are surprising, delightful, original, and reverential. His originality is never egregious: unlike some chefs and bartenders I could name, Gen doesn't create for the sake of trying to appear to be creative. He is exacting, and like the best chefs in Japan, he subtracts what he is making rather than adding to it. He is a minimalist.

There are few guys like Gen: he's fanatical, and as a star he is inspiring.

And while you cannot transform your home or apartment into a Japanese bar scene, you can take time to make a drink rather than focusing primarily on the drinking. This means a smaller pour, use of seasonal ingredients, evocative glass-ware, and maybe even waiting until after dinner to drink.

Throughout US cities, Japanese bars are opening and catching on. One of the best is Angel's Share, just off of Astor Place in Manhattan and hidden up a flight of stairs on the second floor of a small building, behind an unmarked door in a restaurant. Here you can see and enjoy what it's like to be in Japan.

Each of these experiences—tea, coffee, cocktails—have anticipation in common. That waiting and observing deepen taste. By making anticipation as important as fulfillment of desires, we learn more about ourselves, relationships, and surroundings—because we are not yet experiencing satisfaction, we're more alert to possibilities.

Something else just as important, and central to each of these experiences, is silence. Japanese have daily activities that create spaces where words are superfluous. The acts of enjoying tea, coffee, and cocktails in Japan are often accompanied by the guests watching the person making the drinks without saying a word. It's a sign of respect.

Throughout its cities, towns, and villages are tiny cafés, some with as few as three seats at a counter, where it's really quiet. Years ago, my friend Yuko took me to a tearoom attached to a modern art gallery in the Roppongi Hills, around the corner from the enormous and towering Mori building, in which the chief sounds were of water streaming into a long trough (used to clean dishes and cups), the whisking of tea, and whispered conversations. It was hard to believe that this world coincided with the vast capital outside.

You can create these sorts of experiences where you live by setting aside as much time as you can manage and quietly, very quietly, enjoying tea, coffee, or a small drink. Turn off the devices, tune in, and drop out, so to speak. Or better yet, don't speak.

The idea then is to communicate with others through silence.

Go back to a definition of acceptance: "Used by a mother with a child to accept something gently, fun to imagine inside oneself, accepting reality."

Ever see a mother and child in sync with one another? No words are necessary. Words get in the way.

Chapter
Four

Sleep

The boat from Niigata to Sado Island was rocking gently on the Sea of Japan, and Takeshi suggested that we go to a large public room and take a nap.

I've known Takeshi about fifteen years; he's a businessman and a very close friend. We met at *Sake No Jin*, an annual festival in Niigata with nearly one hundred sake producers, where for about ten dollars you can sample as much sake as you like. A number of older men didn't know when to stop drinking and had to be carried out.

Takeshi and I were returning from a day of interviewing people on Sado Island for a few articles I was writing.

The room we entered was the size of a suburban public high school classroom and had no furniture. We faced numerous mats atop thin carpet, occupying every square inch, each of which had on it a neatly folded blanket. A wall of windows facing the slate-colored waters and horizon. Light penetrated through cloudy skies.

I could see a few families and couples and friends sprawled out with belongings at their feet or beside them. About thirty people were in the room—though you would never know that from the silence. It was as quiet as being inside a library: not even a whisper; just the sound of rhythmic breaths of men and women of all ages and children dozing or sound asleep. A few awake read *manga* or played games on cell phones.

We took off our shoes.

Takeshi led us gingerly between mats to a couple of empty ones in a prime location—a corner by the windows. We put down our stuff, I folded up my jacket to use as a pillow and lay down, and very soon my eyes closed. The rocking of the boat on the water lulled me.

I was out.

Sleeping in a room or place filled with strangers is common in Japan. From the exhausted workers bedraggled on the subway having stayed way too late at work (as their bosses demanded) to nap rooms on ferry boats, letting go is part of the culture. The implicit feeling of safety for about *half* the population is part of what adds to the depth of the experience.*

---

* Sexual harassment on subways in the form of groping does occur. It's so bad that there are now "women only" subway cars in Tokyo during rush hours. The *Japan Times* also reported on May 23, 2019, that there is a new anti-groping app available, the Digi Police app, which, "either blasts out a voice shouting 'stop it' at top volume, or produces a full-screen SOS message—which victims can show other passengers—reading: 'There is a molester. Please help.'"

No idealizing of Japan allowed! While most of the time people's privacy and security are respected, immediate work needs to be done in Japan so that positive cultural values are more widespread. The values exist: men need to adhere to them, as do the laws, and men must be prosecuted for violations. What's the point of having laws if they are not enforced? Men need to include women in the group *they* are in, which provides *them* with acceptance. The unhappiness of society is sustained by devaluing others.

Japanese culture has developed extraordinary ways for individuals to establish well-being while still accepting the girdle of social conformity. What these activities have in common is a way to lose oneself—to change one's thinking and feeling through an experience either outside oneself or literally to alter consciousness.

While on the mat en route to Sado, I had feelings that reminded me of having been a child: asleep on the floor, on a mat, in a room of people who were not my family, but who were safe enough to slumber next to for a while. Life seemed richer with possibilities, and I felt a great sense of well-being.

In the United States, we could do more about solving our problems if only we had the energy. When we are overwhelmed, we are too exhausted to do enough about the conditions that create the stress. A tired human being is passive and resigned. To do what's needed to change things that stress us out, we need strength and resilience. And one of the best ways to gain well-being is by checking out.

The 1 percent get their naps. Why not the rest of us? I'm not joking when I say that naps shouldn't be the privilege of the ruling, leisure class.

Kemi Alemoru, writing in dazeddigital.com in June 2018, noted, "The luxury of relaxation is usually reserved for the wealthy and fortunate. A part of the modern aspiration to become rich is that we all dream to one day be able to stop working ourselves to the bone and find more time to rest. There are countless studies highlighting the capitalism-driven epidemic of mass sleep deprivation."

Take naps.

Increasingly, awareness of the power of naps is cropping up. The demands of work and family life all but make this a luxury, but whenever possible, go to sleep.

Put this book down.

Close your eyes.

Take as much time as you can.

I'll wait.

Feeling better?

Research backs up the feeling that naps are beneficial to our physical and mental well-being. I mean, really, it's not rocket science.

Ask a baby.

Dr. Rebecca Spencer, a neuroscientist at the University of Massachusetts in Amherst whose research focuses on sleep, completed a study that, according to an October 2018 BBC article, "appears to be the first to show that naps, and not just overnight sleep, contribute to emotional memory processing in children. . . . In essence, 'kids are really emotional without naps, and they're hypersensitive to emotional stimuli,' she says—because they haven't consolidated the emotional baggage from earlier that day."

Naps enable us to have greater self-control, to take things in, and to accept situations without feeling an impulse to respond to them as if they are urgent or emergencies. That period of reflection grants the well-rested person a refuge from which to observe and perhaps create change.

We all know a person who refers to challenges as crises. Everything's a crisis, an emergency. That individual lacks the consistent ability to take things in, absorb and accept, and include others in decision making. If a person lives in a fantasy world of reactivity, they experience changes in the environment as crises. For that person, a nap is in order, if only for the sake of others subjected to the crisis mode that introduces irrelevant stress. At least others will feel calmer when he or she is asleep.

Most adults, after all, don't throw tantrums, at least not the kind that infants and very young children do from time to time for all sorts of medical, psychological, and situational reasons. But there are those for whom stress is either a modus operandi, a way of life, or some part they've assigned themselves or been assigned in a drama.

The yelling and screaming, accusations, inability to differentiate between the important and the unimportant, and the sheer exhilaration of turning life into a dramatic turn of events makes it hell for those who are sucked into their orbit.

Naps are a surefire way, as with the very young, to turn that incivility into a place of dreams, where nothing stirs and where the cumbersome person can act out their experiences without doing harm to anyone or anything other than bed sheets.

Wouldn't it be nice at the next family get-together to turn to the person who's making others question being there and say, "Take a nap!"

Japan is understandably ambivalent about naps. There is so much pressure from bosses and fellow employees to work long hours that Japanese don't get enough sleep. The postwar mentality is excruciatingly slow to change: rising from literal ashes and becoming a great power, the only Asian member of the G-7, a respected force rather than a feared enemy. The current generation in charge are men over the age of fifty-five whose outlooks and emotional obligations are informed by the traumas and goals of their fathers and grandfathers. So fatigue is viewed as a sign of endurance. If you are so exhausted that you can't keep your eyes open, you've given everything you can.

This outlook will change when one day the generations of the children and grandchildren of the men in charge take over from them. The next generations will implement the values of their experiences, which are different than those preceding them. Until then, rather than change the demands of a long work day, companies are allowing and even encouraging employees to nap on the job.

It's a classic Japanese solution: conflict avoidant. The employer "wins" because people come to work, and employees "win" because they get paid to sleep on company time. Rather than change the context that created the exhaustion, the guys at the top decided to add a nap. Another way to handle this challenge would be to have a shorter work day and lower demands for productivity, but it's always easier to mend a system than to make structural change.

Japan is not a nation heavily invested in Western techniques for identifying or dealing with stress. Diagnostic interviewing, use of antidepressants and other psychotropics, and therapeutic intervention are rare. Yet the rates of depression are about the same as in Western developed nations, and even the reportedly high rate of suicides isn't quite so high: Japan is fourteenth globally at 18.5 percent with France, where joie de vivre is part of a national myth, coming in at seventeenth with 17.7 percent. The United States isn't far behind: twenty-seventh with a rate of 15.3 percent.

In fact, the United States and Japan are about the same on this dire statistic as of 2015: "Based on a survey with some 40,000 valid responses, the number of suicide attempts in 2015 was estimated at around 530,000 (456,000–607,000). There were 24,025 suicides in Japan that year, so it comes out to around 22 attempts for every suicide, which is close to the Centers for Disease Control (CDC) figure of 25 attempts to one suicide in the U.S."*

What this means is that not only doesn't Japan pathologize the expected and necessary challenges of being a human being, but it has other less invasive and more natural ways that people can draw upon to create well-being.

One of these ways is by normalizing the importance of getting enough sleep. The culture is certainly *not* drawing upon its history of sleep and napping as normal, necessary parts of the day, but the fact, ironically, that Japanese can be found asleep in places that would be taboo in the United States suggests that the mechanisms are there for people in Japan to sleep more and work less.

---

*Thanks to Sanja Miklin, PhD candidate in comparative human development at the University of Chicago, who emailed me this data.

It is a nation with the potential to make greater use of sleep. Japanese are not sleeping up to their potential, to paraphrase my tenth grade geometry teacher (who was referring to my apparent unwillingness to demonstrate ability).

They can do it if they want! And so can we.

I've dozed off in Tokyo subways and woken up several stops from my destination, roused by guys in blue uniforms waving white batons, telling all us deadbeats to get out. The last train is at midnight, and the morning trains begin at five a.m., which means that if you're out and about, you might be out and about all night. This is a routine sight in Tokyo because one of the most expensive items in the city is the taxis. It's as if dozens of people are Cinderella, rushing to get home before the trains stop.

I've also shut my eyes at business meetings, just to rest them for a few seconds, only to get a sharp, quick nudge in the ribs from a friend by my side about five minutes into a dreamy state. It's accepted as a sign of my dedication, my perseverance: the guy is tired from jet lag and the twelve or thirteen-hour time difference between Tokyo and the US East Coast, but he showed up! He is so devoted to the work that he is pushing himself to the very limits. Paradoxical, I know.

I've napped in coffee shops, in parks, while waiting on a bench for a counter seat at a noodle shop, and once I nearly dozed off in a hotel lobby and missed the bus that would take me to my flight to Osaka. I wasn't alone; around me people of all ages and genders were checking out.

Hardly anyone gets upset, it's considered part of life, letting go, not being able to attend to matters, just letting the exhaustion take hold. I'm not saying this is ideal, but what I like about it is that no one gets upset about it, except the police on that last train.

Imagine if we all had time to sleep more and work less.

Back home in the States, I take naps late in the afternoon, whenever possible, for fifteen to forty-five minutes, and wake up ready to be part of the world again. I'd love to be able to doze off regularly in public, and the idea of encouraging people to get more sleep as part of a therapeutic plan is a good place to start in diminishing stress.

I know that the people who come to me for help are not getting enough sleep; about 90 percent of the individuals who are evaluated tell me they have trouble falling asleep, have trouble staying asleep, are waking up too early, had a night of bad dreams. The next day is shot. If they found a way to get enough sleep, it would be a whole lot better than invasive techniques. First, try to get some sleep. See how you feel. Still stressed out? Talk about medication with your doctor that might help you. It's not one or the other; it's *when* to ramp things up. Modern medicine works well alongside complementary approaches.

Back in the olden days, before 1937, when the Gross Domestic Production (GDP) was first introduced as a measure of a country's success, people slept more and were less productive.* Once economic growth was introduced as a measure, other experiences that contributed to well-being were devalued.

Japan is no better at resolving this conflict of the GDP as a measure of progress than anywhere else, but here is what is different and what makes resolution more possible: the desire for sleep and the acceptance of napping—its normalization—are part of the Japanese cultural fabric. It's OK to be sleepy; it's normal; it may not require medical intervention.

Now all that needs to be done is: Work less; sleep more.

Easier said than done!

In an article in the *Guardian*, Japanese are described as rather sleepy: "Only 54% of Japanese respondents to the 'bedroom poll' felt they got a good night's sleep every or almost every night."

Inemuri ("sleeping while present"), prevalent in Japan, is a form of sheer exhaustion, and an ironic demonstration that the person who is sleeping in public is so dedicated to the task that they pushed themselves past the limit of consciousness.

As mentioned, I've done it in Japan.

---

*According to the Organization for Economic Cooperation and Development (OECD), "the Gross Domestic Product (GDP) is the standard measure of the value added created through the production of goods and services in a country during a certain period. As such, it also measures the income earned from that production, or the total amount spent on final goods and services (less imports). While GDP is the single most important indicator to capture economic activity, it falls short of providing a suitable measure of people's material well-being for which alternative indicators may be more appropriate."

Wouldn't it be better if the demands of work were lessened? While waiting for that to happen, companies in Japan are co-opting naps. The Japanese government, recognizing the problem and seeing the strategies of companies as viable solutions, is encouraging naps as well. Numerous companies in Japan now have napping rooms and siesta times; this may seem generous, and perhaps it is, but the bottom line is that the employee does not leave work.

"Sleep debt" was "one of Japan's top buzzwords in 2017."

People in power are willing to work their employees to the point of exhaustion. Just to be clear: It isn't as if the men at the top are taking long vacations and getting enough shut-eye either. It is a symptom of Japan's decades-long, mad, national rush to create one of the world's economic powerhouses. Something had to be sacrificed in order for Japan to take its "rightful place" among the powerful Western nations. Many Japanese figured that they would sleep when they were dead. What mattered more than their personal fatigue was overcoming the shame of wartime defeat through hard work.

Well, that plan for becoming a world power, side by side with the postcolonial and powerful West, served its purpose, I guess, and then in 2017 or thereabouts, sleep-deprived Japanese basically said that while not sleeping enough was OK for their fathers and grandfathers, they needed more rest.

Companies in Japan came up with innovative ways to enable people to sleep at work. "Tokyo-based Nextbeat Co. set up two so-called 'strategic sleeping rooms'—one for female and one for male workers. "Property developer Mitsubishi

Estate Co. . . . also established three napping rooms each for men and women." It's not just about *helping* people rest up as a humane gesture. Companies are seeing the monetary costs of exhaustion.

"Nao Tomono, a sleep consultant who taught seminars for the Sompo Japan Nipponkoa Himawari Life Insurance Inc. (which provided their workers a portable device that can gauge the length and depth of sleep), said, 'There is a growing importance to re-examining sleep since low work efficiency and mental and physical disorders lead to big economic losses.'"[*]

Industry leaders in the United States share the concerns of their Japanese counterparts. According to *Inc.* magazine, "lack of sleep costs U.S. companies a staggering $63 billion in productivity." So of course some companies are doing something about it.

The website sleep.org. notes that Ben & Jerry's, Zappos, Nike, and NASA, among many others, provide nap rooms for their workers. The best known proponent of napping at work is Google. According to a CBS News report, at Google there are "on-site sleep pods, complete with cashmere eye masks. As David Radcliffe, VP of real estate and workplace services at Google, said in an interview with CBS, 'No workplace is complete without a nap pod.'" And Ariana Huffington and others have started companies that

---

[*] From *Japan Times*. "Japanese Firms Starting to Encourage Employees to Take Naps at Work." November 22, 2018.

rent mattresses and rooms for daytime dozing. Calling her company Thrive Global, Ms. Huffington notes that "87% of employees worldwide are not engaged at work, 78% of companies identify stress as a top workplace health risk, and 96% of senior leaders report feeling burned out."

Americans are exhausted. While the economic costs are staggering, the health risks are so important that the Centers for Disease Control (CDC) examined the problem and found, according to a study released in February 2016, that "more than a third of American adults are not getting enough sleep on a regular basis."

Think of how you feel and act at work and with your loved ones when you don't get enough sleep. Chances are you're irritable, reactive, angry, miserable, and unfocused. Consider that you're not the only one who's sleepy. What then?

We're living in communities of stressed out Americans. If you want to know what *contributes* to the current national mess we're in, look at sleeplessness. If Americans got more sleep, we would have more energy upon waking up, requisite for changing the relationships we have and the things that keep us up at night.

And of course those who are most disenfranchised, who have the least authority, also have the least sleep. The CDC study notes that "healthy sleep duration was lower among Native Hawaiians/Pacific Islanders (54 percent), non-Hispanic blacks (54 percent), multiracial non-Hispanics (54 percent) and American Indians/Alaska Natives (60 percent) compared with non-Hispanic whites (67 percent), Hispanics (66 percent), and Asians (63 percent)." The CDC found that "short sleep duration," less than seven hours per night, was highest among black Americans (45.8 percent) and lowest among white Americans (33.4 percent).

Sleep has become a commodity, even a luxury, and if you can afford it, you can have more of it. Exhaustion isn't affecting all of us in the same way.

There are reasons why some of us are well rested and others of us are tired all or most of the time. In his book *The Happiness Fantasy*, Carl Cederström cites Jonathan Crary, author of *24/7: Late Capitalism and the Ends of Sleep*: "Jonathan Crary argues that capitalism now seeks to colonize people at all times, including when they sleep. In the United States, he claims, the average person has gone from sleeping ten hours at the beginning of the twentieth century, to eight hours in the 1950s, to six and a half hours today. . . . Sleep is threatened with subordination to the logic of productivity."

Cederström refers to the work of Byung-Chul Han, a professor at the Berlin University of the Arts and author of *The Burnout Society*: "When every moment is translated into an opportunity to make yourself more productive or more effective, then there are no longer any pockets of unproductive time, outside of capitalist accumulation. This obsession with achievement and activeness is 'generating excessive tiredness and exhaustion.' Worse, it is a solitary tiredness. It has, Han continues, 'a separating and isolating effect.'"

Let's hope you are lucky enough to work for a company that pays you to nap on the job. Then, when you wake up feeling well-rested, you can think of ways to get better working conditions and higher wages so you won't need to nap quite so much.

Naps are a way to accept life's problems and say, "You know what? I'm checking out for a while. I am taking a nap. No more work."

So I'm not advocating naps in order for you to produce more, although if you want to add purpose to one of the most blissfully purposeless activities we can engage in, feel free. I see naps more the way that Clinton sees them.

Clinton is my cat, a homeless street veteran of the Lower East Side of Manhattan (named after a street there), and she naps most of the day. She is by far one of the most relaxed living creatures I have ever met. Talk about well-being. She lies on her back, paws in the air, her body in a state of extreme repose, looking as if she has been washed ashore. No thought of being more productive; on the contrary, it's the last thing on her mind.

Be more like Clinton, I tell myself.

And you can be like her, too.

Chapter Five

Soaked

Is there such a thing as the cleanest, most well-scrubbed people on earth? If only research existed on the subject, we might find out. What we do know is that Japan is trying, as a nation, to bathe life's dirt, actual and spiritual, away. People in Japan love to soak. Holidays are organized at *onsen* and *ryokan*, where entire generations of families get into hot water, naked head to toe, usually segregated by gender, to sit back, eyes closed, and accept nature's embrace. Then, too, public baths, which once proliferated in US cities, provide the opportunity to bathe nude beside neighbors and strangers, and the shame of exposure really does lessen or even go away.

Talk about the acceptance of *ukeireru*!

Bathing is de rigueur in Japan, and whenever possible people there are in hot water or thinking about getting into hot water. It starts in the morning in a tub, at home or in a public bath, with buckets you pour over your head. And it ends after a day of work, when, bedraggled and worn out, you soak in a tub.

When staying at *ryokan*, the inns throughout the country, I take baths in each property's hot springs with other naked

guests before breakfast, after breakfast, after lunch, before
dinner, and after dinner.

Many cultures place a value on public and private baths.
Japan is not alone, but there is a huge difference between
bathing in Japan and how it's done elsewhere.

Ancient Greeks and then Romans turned bathing into a
cornerstone of their sybaritic culture. The well-to-do back
then enjoyed an excess of pleasure in exclusive retreats.*

That's really the point: bathing in ancient times and up
to the present day in many societies was and is the province
of the upper classes, a sliver of entitlement, and a symbol of
wealth. Who else has the time and money to spend soaking?

In Western Europe, it became an industry. Inspired by
writers who placed spa towns in novels, and travel companies
promoting visits to hot springs resorts, a high-end market
developed, from Marienbad to Aix les Bains to Leukerbad
to Vichy.†

"Taking the cure" was how they put it in the nineteenth
and early twentieth centuries. You went to soak away life's
stressors (or major medical problems, like tuberculosis, in-

---

*Taking a page from this extraordinary decadence, a US company based in
Minnesota ("Land of 10,000 Lakes"), has named itself after the way of life
in Sybaris, an ancient Greek settlement in southern Italy: Sybaritic. Sign up
with it, and get your own private pod where you can, according to its website, "Become one with water." The Sybaritic Relaxwell Oceanpod caught
my eye: it's sleek, beautiful to look at, and at $23,995 the best Christmas
present *ever* if my wife is reading this and wants to take out a loan.

† You can still luxuriate in elite spas, like the gorgeous baths in Vals, Switzerland, designed by Peter Zumthor, winner of the Pritzker, the most
prestigious award in architecture. Or visit any number of upscale retreats
in Europe and North America.

curable before antibiotics). Little was said about the causes of stress, and the aim was to be "cured" by a willful forgetting that would be inspired by long soaks in outdoor and indoor baths fed by natural hot springs.

But there was another side to bathing. Immigrants coming to the United States, and working people in European cities, lived head to toe in rooms or apartments that did not have showers or baths. You can still see remnants of public baths on New York's Lower East Side.

When I was a kid, my dad took me to a public bath (a *schvitz*, a place of sweat, he called it) in the Garment District of Manhattan, and it was in a deep subterranean floor of a nondescript building, filled with big, old, oversized men, naked and wobbling, stepping in and out of hot baths on slippery tiles. They weren't silent, they groaned a lot, and the sound was like nothing I'd heard before: familiar was the expression of relief and even a bit of pleasure; unfamiliar was the unmistakable ooze of sadness. Between baths, we sat in a wet room with a tier of wooden benches, and some men hit themselves with long, leafy, aromatic oak branches. If I close my eyes and sit still awhile, I can imagine the smell of the leaves and the sweat of the tired men.

What happens in Japan isn't typically elite, nor is it a life apart. Just about every community has a public bath where there is an opportunity to really get to know who's who and to show the world who you are, too. You accept your flawed nakedness; you accept the nakedness of others.

It's difficult to be intimidated by fancy-pants people when bathing next to them without their pants on.

At one particular *ryokan* where I have stayed many times, the owner is a very distinguished gentleman in his eighties with a taut bearing and an ability to make others around him feel small. When we have met over the years and talked about the history he has lived through, as well as his travels and his knowledge, I've been tongue-tied.

It wasn't until recently, when he entered the bathing area coincidentally at the same time I was there, threw off his *yukata*, and exposed his thin, wiry, pale body, dunking a bucket of water over his head and then joining me in the hot water, that I felt comfortable being with him.

Japan, as a whole, has recognized for centuries the myriad benefits to be had by taking hot baths with others in the community.

Let me give you an even more personal example of what I'm talking about, and how bathing is experienced in Japan today.

Recently, I was having dinner at an *izayaka* with Hiro, an old friend. We had met at a food conference ages ago, through mutual friends. Passionate about food, which he calls his religion, Hiro got a degree in political science from Waseda University in Tokyo, but nowadays he designs websites for Japanese companies that do business in the West.

Hiro and I had just polished off about eight courses of small bites: grilled salmon, fresh tofu with sansho peppers, steamed sweet potatoes, and so forth.

"I want to tell you about my new hobby," Hiro said.

He's a man of few words, so I knew that the beer and sake we had also consumed would fuel what he was about to say.

"Oh?" I said.

"Yes," he said.

We ate and drank more in silence.

"Your hobby," I said, after awhile.

"Mmm," he said between bites. "Yes, my hobby."

I waited.

"I like spas," he said.

"Spas?"

"Yes, I started going a few times a week to different ones around town," he said. "I find the experience to be very relaxing."

"How long do you go for each visit?"

"Three hours, on average," he said.

"Three hours?"

"Mmm, hmm."

"What are they like?"

He explained.

"OK," I said, "Let's go."

"Tonight?!" He made an open expression of surprise and delight. "Great!"

So after dinner Hiro hailed a cab, and we wound through the wide avenues around Shinjuku train station, then into alleyways, until he told the driver to stop in front of a long row of tall, gray buildings that looked like they contained small offices.

We got out and Hiro began to search. Strict rules exist about size and appearance of signage in Japan, so even locals can have difficulties finding what they are looking for. Finally, we came upon a long, vertical panel of names with the one we were looking for, and we rode up in a four-person elevator.

The door slid open on the tenth floor, which was for men only. (The ninth floor was for women only.)

It wasn't at all what I expected.

A tiny foyer housed a check-in area, where a man stood behind a counter. For a thousand Japanese yen, about ten dollars, we were each given a key to a locker and an hour in which to enjoy ourselves.

After each of us stripped off our clothes and locked them up, Hiro and I walked down a short hallway and pushed open a door to the baths.

In a room that was about the size of four freight elevators, there was a cold bath, a hot bath, a few lounge chairs, and a dry sauna. All around us were nearly two dozen men, old and young, unembarrassed, nonchalant, as if it was the most natural thing in the world to lounge around naked among strangers.

It wasn't a sexualized place; it was just a place to let go, to embrace the strange comfort that can come about through this level of extreme vulnerability.

We stayed the hour, no one spoke around us, and I dozed awhile in a lounge chair between periods of immersing myself in water.

After the baths, Hiro showed me a small lounge near the reception desk where, for around 1,500 yen, we could have a beer, soft drink, or whisky and snacks. Next to this area was a darkened room with cots. Men could stay the night for about 3,000 yen.

This wasn't a flophouse or SRO: the walls were lined with framed and autographed photographs of some of Japan's most famous baseball players. Like at most of the spas, Hiro explained, all sorts of people, from businessmen to celebrities, stopped in.

"The ballplayers often come here to relax," explained Hiro. "And you can find at least one of these spas next to every subway stop. There must be at least one thousand in Tokyo alone, some just for men, some just for women."

I'm not sure at all if these sorts of businesses will crop up outside of Japan, though I'm told that you can see them starting in some US cities, like San Francisco, but I can see why it is my friend's hobby. I experienced vulnerability while still feeling safe. And it was a way to shut off the outside world. In the spa, stimuli were cut back; it was restful, quiet, and idle.

In many public baths, Japanese show up with little bags that hold towels and cosmetics and whatnot. Unlike a *schvitz*, there is no moaning or groaning, and people are usually quiet. There's not a whole lot of acknowledged shame to being naked in a bath with a group of people; it's accepted as a natural way of life. Yet another way to accept being part of an established group.

Japan has geothermal energy, so natural hot water in which to soak away troubles can be found readily. This, too, is a form of acceptance: nature isn't going to get less violent; there will always be earthquakes and volcanoes in Japan. So accept the gifts of hot springs that these otherwise powerful and deadly natural features can offer you.

Ultimately, the number one feature of Japan's culture of bathing, which we can learn from, is its demotic quality. Bathing in Japan is popular and meant to be enjoyed by everyone. It's not just for elites, and it's not only for the urban poor.*

Naked men and women, bare breasted or bare chested, are required to make use of a small towel to cover genitals when walking from the (required) showers or wooden buckets of water to the hot springs.

You clean up before and after the bath with soaps and shampoos; in the bath you simply soak. Once you are immersed in the hot springs, put the towel, folded neatly, on your head or beside the pools.

There you are, up to your neck, eyes closed, maybe whispering with a friend, trying as best you can not to "be one with the water," or "taking the cure," but really and truly feeling as close to nature as you can. Many of the baths, at *onsen* and in communities, are bordered by rocks and in forests; surrounded by open air, the sounds of birds, breezes through trees, and there are few things more sensational than immersion in the water while snow falls or heavy rain pounds down.

---

*There are caveats. Tattoos are pretty much taboo in baths in Japan, even in hotels and inns, as Japanese associate these with membership in *yakuza*, which are organized crime syndicates. *Yakuza* savor tattoos, and if you are a Westerner in Japan with a tattoo you may be denied entry to a bath or be given a bandage to cover up (if it's small enough, like the tumbling dice on my left bicep, to be covered).

Essentially, there are two ways to bathe in Japan. You can bathe alone, and you can bathe in a group of friends or strangers. Both have extraordinary merits.

One of the most memorable bathing experiences I had in my life was in a small, sunken pool at the Kayotei *ryokan*. It was before dawn, and no one else was up. I was jet-lagged and shuffled barefoot through chilly corridors on *tatami* mats that had an aroma of rice straw, then down a short flight of steps to the baths. I removed my *yukata*. Wooden buckets and a flat wooden stool, low to the ground, were positioned in front of faucets, and I rinsed before stepping into the water. In front of the bath was a wall of glass, which had a latch for the floor-to-ceiling center window. Undoing the latch, I slid the window back. Snow poured in. I could also hear snowflakes falling on black branches. Gradually, as it got light, and as I sat in the bath, the forest appeared. I was alone but part of nature, so not alone.

Another time, I bathed with a group of strangers, Japanese and Westerners, outside of Myojinkan *ryokan* in Matsumoto, most of us whispering and laughing, just enjoying being together in the hot water. Feeling a sense of belonging I had not felt before.

Studies support these anecdotes. You can find research describing lower blood pressure, less arthritic pain, softer skin, and mental calm by bathing in natural hot springs. The hard data isn't conclusive, and it's not at all evident that the effects are lasting. But that's not entirely the point.

Bathing calms you down, it *does* offer a cure of sorts, and you don't need a doctor to tell you when something feels good. This information is a bonus, like finding out that scientists have learned that chocolate cake is not just delicious but good for you.

Lately, there's a trend to bring bathing into the lives of more people, up close and direct. One of the biggest proponents of this is the forest bathing movement, epitomized by Shinrin Yoku (shinrin-yoku.org). The website notes that forest bathing helps you to "Breathe, Relax, Wander, Touch, Listen, Heal."[*]

Up to Our Necks in Hot Water

From a more entrepreneurial standpoint, and if you're too far from a forest, cropping up lately in cities and towns throughout the West are renovated public baths that offer peaceful soaks.[†]

In Europe, you'll find spas that have Roman-Irish baths, which invite men and women to walk around naked together, going from bath to bath of varying temperatures, in silence,

---

[*] M. Amos Clifford is the person behind forest bathing, and he has a long history of commitment to therapeutic work as well as a love of nature. He had the creative ability to combine these skills. What's fascinating about Clifford's background is his work in therapeutic change. This is about acceptance of self in nature and experiencing ourselves as part of nature, and just as importantly there is recognition that this is where we belong.

[†] One company cashing in on the trend is AIRE Ancient Baths (beaire .com/en), which has baths in Manhattan, Barcelona, Chicago, London, and Paris.

to try to soak away troubles. Having done this, I can tell you that it's an unforgettable way to get to know your neighbors.

These baths put us in touch with our bodies, with nature, and with others in our communities. It's humbling to sit still and immerse oneself in water without saying very much. The water takes over, and it is a way to change our thoughts and emotions, and to accept our place in the world, exposed and vulnerable.

And Now Let Us Bathe

Every religion recognizes the power of bathing as a way to bring us closer to things outside ourselves.

The ritual of baptism in Christianity. The *mikvah* or ritual baths of Judaism. The annual ritual bathing in Hinduism of *Magh Mela* for purposes of purification, and the importance of daily bathing known as *snanam*. In Islam, there is *ghusl* bathing for purification. Each of these carry a connotation of guilt and shame and are wrapped up in condemnation of sexuality.

But while modern bathing may be rooted in some twisted ways to washing away one's sins, it has more in common with the way the ancients did it: a celebration of our bodies, in water, alone or with friends and strangers, closer to our souls and nature than when we are clothed.

Japanese are not an especially religious society these days and are far more spiritual than fearful of a deity or devoted to appeasing gods through prayer and obedience. What we can take from their approach is an understanding that if we know what nature expects of us, we are better able to accept it and ourselves.

Some of the time, I feel as if I'm in hot water because I've failed or disappointed myself and others, and that decision to embrace failure and self-loathing creates stress. But once I'm actually *in* hot water, whatever it is that frightens me and makes me miserable seems less intense. Not a cure, but a respite.

Chapter Six

What Is Nature?

Japanese, worshipful and respectful of nature to the point that aspects of self-identity are defined by being in gardens and forests, in the mountains, and by the sea, have at the same time an inability to resist the urge to destroy that which sustains them.

Japan is a leader among industrialized nations in environmental degradation, from whale hunting to toxins in the soil to pollutants in the air to the transformation of arable land into industrial wastelands.

The rush after the war to build an economy that could compete globally and that would perhaps make up for the humiliation of defeat motivated Japanese governments and companies to prioritize growth over protecting nature. It seemed more important to rebuild the nation than to act responsibly toward the environment. This painful decision was at odds with a much older ethos of worshipping nature that characterizes Japanese life.

In addition to environmental damage done willfully, Japanese, as we all know, suffered destruction by outside forces. During the Second World War, US bombing raids, which included the horrifying and inhumane atomic attacks on the civilian populations of Hiroshima and Nagasaki, as well as firestorms from carpet bombings in Tokyo, flattened most of its major cities.

In the context of these traumas, its cities are buttressed and seemingly prepared for the worst, with deep centers far below the earth's surface with subterranean street names and a multitude of shops. As if to provide shelter where life could continue in places that are unnatural, and where everything is man-made, should that become necessary.

To make matters worse, natural disasters result in shocking devastation: the Great Kanto Earthquake in Tokyo in 1923, the Kobe earthquake of 1995, the Tōhoku (Sendai) earthquake and subsequent tsunami of 2011, and numerous fires in Kyoto throughout the centuries. Historically, because of a violent geography, countless, horrifying, and sudden catastrophes took place with grim regularity. And still do.

Urban centers in Japan are filled with tall steel, glass, and concrete buildings, designed to withstand earthquakes and tidal waves, supposed to last forever. They are anything but arcadian and instill a feeling of being lost. That sense of abandonment, and separation from the natural world, is worsened by the extraordinary difficulty of getting around.

As Ted Bestor noted in his classic work *Neighborhood Tokyo*, streets and building numbers are in disarray. The markers are not always in order; signs are often absent. It's not unusual to be with locals walking or in taxis when the person gets on their cell phone and calls someone at the destination point in order to be guided to a place only a block or two away.

But at the same time as one sees this chaos, and disregard or alienation, there is a serene and ineradicable feeling among Japanese that human beings are defined by nature. There's a sense that our anxieties and sadness, our difficulty in accepting life's brevity, come about because we have lost our place in the natural order of things. And that with effort and diligence, through practice, we can restore ourselves and establish well-being by trying to figure out and accept what nature expects of us.

The experience of trauma and the heated, industrialized reactions to it, the way many Japanese in cities are cut off from nature, heighten the strong need to renew the traditional attachments. These ties were damaged or lost, and nowadays Japanese strive to bring them back. The struggle or tension between modernity and preservation defines, in large measure, contemporary Japanese culture.

This outlook on life—restoring balance between the perks of the modern world with nature—is really an *individual* phenomenon, especially in privileged nations.

How many people have given up streaming video, iPhones, online retail, and virtual reality, or any of the numerous things that make life so much easier than it was for all of the other previous generations?

That's right, I said it: easier.

In numerous ways that hardly bear repeating, but just in case there's any doubt, many of us get more things done over the Internet in minutes that used to take hours and days, from renewing a driver's license to renting a car to buying a pair of pants. Not having to run around to offices and stores means that I have more time to do things that seem to have greater value. I'm one of those people who doesn't see the downside of technology but rather views it as an incredibly helpful set of tools used to solve problems. And, yes, OK, I spend too much time on the Internet, just like many others, because, wait, *did you see what he just tweeted?*

What?!

But I also spend many weeks each year deep in the mountains, looking at clouds, cows, trees, and birds. It really is possible to have both, and why not, if you're lucky enough to have both?

Japanese try to have economic growth along with a desire to fit in with nature's expectations. To accommodate modernity with tradition, to provide an economic infrastructure for future generations while simultaneously preserving and worshipping nature that makes life worthwhile and meaningful. How do Japanese go about this uniquely? In places where the old and the new rub up against each other in Japan, it is possible to feel the tension most powerfully. Through that feeling, awareness and maybe even insight come about.

I have felt that level of tension in Kyoto, which was bombed during the Second World War approximately five times. As a result of having been nearly spared by US air force bombings, a lot of its architecture, from Gion to its modern districts, is very traditional or old fashioned. In 2007, the city passed an ordinance limiting buildings to about ten stories and banned all rooftop advertising signs and blinking lights. Dozens of ancient shrines and temples are found throughout the city. Famous, tiny *ryokan* can be found in back streets and alleyways. Many Japanese are out and about in kimonos and wooden clogs. There are centuries-old teahouses, soba shops, and tofu stands. In and around the open-air Nishiki market are many artisan shops selling museum-quality lacquerware, fans, and textiles. It's not hard to imagine what Kyoto may have looked like a century ago.

Kyoto also possesses very cool brew pubs, lots of Western tourists and students, a thriving contemporary art scene, good Italian restaurants, a subway system, jazz clubs, and big department stores. The city is in the middle of a luxury hotel boom with international brands opening up to cash in on what travel magazines are naming "the World's Best City."

Locals worry that Kyoto is turning into the Japanese Venice or Barcelona, a Disneyfied version of what makes it a remarkable place. No place is more vibrant, and the clash here has clues we can interpret in order to acquire well-being in our lives through acceptance of nature.

In 2017, I began work with Ken Yokoyama, the former general manager of Hyatt Regency Kyoto, on an exciting project that would open up Zen Buddhist temples to Westerners for extended stays.

My task was to write about the temples for a new website. A monk at each temple was in charge of greeting the visitors, offering talks about Zen, and teaching meditation, and I was asked to interview these men in order to document their histories and beliefs for prospective guests.

Five properties were selected. Quarters where monks had once lived were renovated and now had ultra-modern, fully equipped kitchens, big bedrooms, deep wooden tubs, long corridors of polished wooden planks, big windows, and bare wooden walls. These digs had views of private gardens with manicured trees and shrubs; a couple of the gardens also had ponds in which koi swam and cranes dived.

Guests had private access to the temples at each site, daily *zazen* meditation lessons with a monk, and opportunities to learn firsthand about the rituals associated with a lifestyle created by acceptance of life's ephemerality.

It was very intimidating to spend an hour or two with each monk. I had read a lot about Zen Buddhism in the months before the job began, in order to prepare for the interviews, but once I was face-to-face with the monks, the task before me was scary. I didn't want to sound like an idiot: worshipful, ignorant, disrespectful.

I probably sounded like an idiot. But maybe less of an idiot than I would have had I not been aware of not wanting to sound like one. I wasn't sure what to ask, so I would start by thanking the monk for wasting his time with me and then would ask very open-ended questions: How long have you lived here? What is your day like? When did you decide to become a monk?

Once we had established affiliation, the talks became relaxed and conversational, and the monks told me personal things about themselves.

One monk had lived in California for decades working as a real estate investor and restaurant entrepreneur. He returned to Kyoto to accept the mantle of head monk at a temple when his father, the former head monk, had died. He was a terrific mix of suave, laid-back West Coast vibe and Japanese spirituality.

One monk said that he had not left the compound for decades. Another worked with his son cooking meals for foreign guests based on ancient precepts. A fourth monk showed me a book written about his teachings by a professor at Columbia University. The fifth monk spoke a lot in parables and had a great sense of humor.

Each man would talk at length, very slowly, and I took notes. Usually, we started interviews on *tatami* mats, shoes off, resting on bent feet tucked, a difficult posture that gave me cramps in both ankles since I hadn't sat like that my whole life. So then I'd sit cross-legged and rub my ankles until the pain went away.

We drank green tea. After our talks, the monks showed me gardens, reliquaries, and the temple interior.

Even though the men were middle-aged or old, each of them moved with a deliberate, adroit, and elastic manner suggestive of athleticism. Then, too, when they sat, they *sat*. They *really* sat. They sat without moving a muscle. In their movements and stillness, the level of self-control and concentration was new to me and like nothing I had seen close up before.

When they spoke, it was with precise brevity, as if each word was an intrusion upon the natural sounds around us. The words also disrupted the unspoken connection we were trying to establish with one another.

It wasn't as if the monks knew more about life. From their perspective, from the standpoint of Zen, it was as if they knew *less*: everything about their manner suggested that being analytical was a barrier. It was best to accept nature, to be part of it, to sort out what nature expected of us rather than try to impose ourselves. And that process started (and ended) with letting go.

"You have to free your mind," Shodo Egami, the monk at Shinnyoji Temple, told me. He was the funny guy who spoke in parables. "To have no mind. To experience."

The concept, let alone the way of life it created for the monks, was alien, but in the short time I stayed at the temple where Ken had assigned me, it grew on me, and very slowly I felt less intimidated by these holy men.

It helped that Ken, whom I've known for close to twenty years, has a wry sense of irreverence cultivated from working a long time in Australia and with Westerners. And the fact that his undergraduate degree is in American literature. He told me his favorite writer is Mark Twain and his favorite book is *The Adventures of Huckleberry Finn*.

We were enjoying a steak dinner and good French red wine, after my day spent in the temple, as a debriefing.

"That's what Egami-san said to you?" Ken asked between bites. He has a really big smile, and with his shaved head, he looks like a Buddha after slimming down. "Really? And you bought it?"

"Well, yeah, Ken, why? What, is this some kind of test?" I laughed. "You don't take these guys seriously? I mean, you're the one who's always telling me about how important

Buddhist traditions are to you and your family. And how you want to preserve the pre-Western ways of Japan. So which is it?"

"Both," he said. He smiled. "Don't take it too seriously."

"It?"

"The whole thing," he said.

"So you don't believe what the monks are saying?"

He just shook his head like an old friend playing a trick on yet another Westerner seeking enlightenment in all the wrong places.

"*Sumimasen!*" Ken shouted to get the attention of a waiter who came running to our table as if it was an emergency. "Wine, *Onegaishimasu.*"*

"I'm not talking about belief," he said, as we drank more wine. Ken knows his wines. "The monks live well. Live well, too. Why not?"

I woke up each morning in what had once been the monks' quarters of the Kouunji Temple. My room had a wall of sliding-glass doors that faced a garden, and down the hall was a square cedar tub I filled with hot water for a long soak. After a bath, I would go to a garden next to the property's kitchen and stand around awhile with a cup of coffee listening to breezes coursing through the forest on the hills above us.

Before meeting Ken and a monk for the day's interview, I would often stroll on the famous *Tetsugaku no Michi* (Philosopher's Path) alongside Biwa Canal, which were about

---

*The word for "wine" in Japanese is . . . wine.

fifteen feet from where I was staying. The path led to Zen Buddhist temples and Shinto shrines. Plum and cherry trees lined the canal. It was February: plum blossoms. Tall, ancient oaks with long branches stood in the Shinto compounds; the Zen temples had manicured gardens.

All this meant something. A way of observing, to be sure, but also well-being. I didn't feel so alone, even though I *was* alone. My wife and kids were in the States. And the weird thing, the really weird thing, was that in the evenings when I met Japanese friends in town for drinks and *yakitori*, *that* was when I felt alone, *that* was when loneliness and sadness crept in with familiarity, making themselves right at home. It was lonelier being with friends than with nature.

Having the opportunity to see and feel life inside a Zen temple compound, walking along a path to Shinto shrines and other temple sites, feeling blissfully insignificant. What I felt and thought, for the time being, mattered less than what I saw around me. It was reassuring to know that nature defined me rather than anything I might accomplish, liberating in the sense that I was free to observe without authority. To try to accept my helplessness.

I thought a lot about what Ken said. It reminded me of a wintry afternoon with my friend Takeshi some years before. He had driven us to a pond near rice paddies a few miles from his apartment in Niigata to look at migratory birds. I had started to tell him a Zen *koan* that seemed to fit the setting, and he had laughed, too.

"Oh no!"

"What?" I said.

"A Western guy telling me a Zen *koan?!* No!" He started giggling. "No, please, not a Zen *koan!*"

"Alright, fine," I said.

"Good."

"So a son asks his father, who is a famous thief, how to break into houses. . . ."

Takeshi let me tell him the *koan*—he's that tolerant a friend—but he had made his point, as had Ken. Buddhist wisdom is a full-blown orientation, a totality, a way of seeing, and nature was what gave it legitimacy. It wasn't a set of commandments; there really wasn't a gospel; people didn't have little Buddha figures as pendants linked to chains around their necks. What the monks were saying was telegraphic, which is: find your position in nature, change your life, and discover where you fit in.

Yes, the industrialization and pressure to spend more time in office cubicles is terrible. Which is why the value of being in nature increases. The more you experience that value, the less important being away from it seems. And it is highly specific: nature's brevity, its indifference to you, the way things go on as if you're not there, as if you don't matter.

Well, you *don't* matter, none of us do, and oddly enough that means far less stress—what you *do* needs to adhere to nature, not to your *idea* of its importance. You don't get to decide. Soon enough none of us will be here.

Which, as I integrated these thoughts derived from Japanese ways of seeing nature, made the frustrations and annoyances of everyday life seem far less important.

If we move beyond identity based on self-fulfillment, and see how it's nature that determines our existence, we get new perspectives on what creates happiness.

Ken was right: "Don't take it too seriously."

In order to diminish the impact of loneliness, the long hours at work, the degradation of the environment, the awareness of being cut off from nature that these experiences entail, it is necessary—and lucky—to find peace of mind in the natural world.

Most Japanese are not fortunate enough to spend time in a Zen temple retreat, have mornings in a garden, or take strolls each day through Shinto shrines. But the information associated with each of these is embedded in Japanese consciousness.

I have taken these experiences and dwell in them as much as possible here in the States. Even in an urban parking lot, I see tall, wild grass with more clarity—the resilience of nature. Or on a walk with my Bernese mountain dog, Beau, early in the morning, way before the city neighborhood is roused, the cries of the blue jays and the swooping hawk and the rabbits hopping for cover all take up more time in my thoughts than before. I find it's easier and paradoxically more relaxing to worry about the prey and to feel the sadness of the cardinal's color changing seasonally than to think about myself. These natural things matter more, and although my awareness of them is unintegrated, not part of my self-identity *yet*, I'm trying hard to create and build a way of seeing myself as part of nature in the Japanese tradition.

What for me is a cultural experience is for Japanese a way of life. Whether Japanese are at a rave club or stuck at their desks past midnight, so exhausted that they might collapse, there remains the feeling that something is not right: the industrialized world does not have all the answers, and before Japan chose to modernize in order to avoid colonization by the West, it was defined by attachment to nature. That awareness is played out in activities still extant in ordinary homes and lives.

Although most Japanese are not daily practitioners of the Zen Buddhist or Shinto religions, many make pilgrimages to temples and shrines yearly or seasonally. So take the time where you live to mark the seasons in places that bring them to life and make you feel part of the world. Whether it's leaf peeping in New England, going to the Cloisters in New York City, or visiting a park, go outdoors, and do nothing but take things in. How do you fit in with what you see? What's your part in all of this?

Mental and physical health are so closely linked to experiencing nature each day that city programs are instituting the practice. So if you can't organize it on your own, those in charge of public infrastructure are creating opportunities for you.

The *New York Times* journalist Jane Brody noted, "In partnership with the National Recreation and Parks Association and Urban Land Institute, the Trust for Public Land started a noble initiative that could bring Minneapolis-type benefits to every resident in the country: access to 'a high quality park within a 10-minute, or half-mile walk."

The idea is to establish natural centers in urban communities where people can clear their heads and observe nature. It's catching on: Brody wrote that more than 220 mayors support the project, "which has as much potential to do as much or more for the nation's physical and mental health than anything Congress might pass." The benefits of experiencing nature are put forward to justify the expansion of the initiative: "A 10-minute walk can enhance physical fitness, reduce the risk of chronic disease and improve brain function, like learning and memory."

Dr. Hanaa Hamdi, the Trust for Public Land's public health director, makes it all sound so genuinely appealing that it makes me wonder why companies, mental hospitals, and communities don't make being outdoors part of schedules. According to the article, Dr. Hamdi's, "research has shown that community green spaces can reduce violent crime; counter stress and social isolation, especially for older adults; improve concentration for children with attention deficit disorder; enhance relaxation; and promote self-esteem and resilience."

Actually, income parity, access to good health care, fair and diverse education, and safe housing are more likely responsible for improvement in each of these areas than trees. But there is no doubt that being in nature is both calming and restorative, so much so that it can give people the requisite energy, well-being, and insight needed to change the causes of their stress.

When you are in nature, try not to talk about work or what's gone wrong or where you're headed. Observe what's around you as silently as possible. The historian Theodore Roszak called it "ecopsychology," and the idea is to let nature dictate the terms, to create experiences that bring individuals face-to-face with nature without anyone or anything interpreting the meaning.

Japanese excel at gardens, and if you are capable, start cultivating.

The urban garden movement is growing day by day in the United States. In major cities throughout the country, plots of land are being made available for people to grow vegetables. With your hands dirty, your body close to the soil, you might begin to rethink your priorities.

Start early.

Alice Waters, with her Edible Schoolyard program, has shown that kids love eating what they grow, and being out in the fresh air and eating healthy food are of benefit to their emotional well-being. Most rewarding of all is the act of taking care of something that depends on us for survival. It's great to teach kids that empathy is part of their education in school. Maybe this will cut down on selfishness; after all, I never saw Ayn Rand's *Book of Gardening*.

Adapting specific Japanese appreciation for gardens with the American Way of Life is one approach to greater well-being. I'm not saying that flower arranging is going to catch on here, but the attentiveness, precision, and slowness of that activity associated with being in nature are real methods for calming the nerves.

Japanese also make note of twenty-four very short seasons, known as *sekki*, some lasting only a few days. Because of the brevity, the observer has to pay close attention or will miss out. You've got periods known as *keichitsu*, when insects wake up from winter hibernation. *Shoshu*, when summer heat is forgotten. *Kokuu*, when it's the start of spring rain needed to begin planting.

Take the time to do something with nature—anything—that involves interacting with what you see and hear. It could be watching birds and learning their calls, or getting to know the types of trees in your neighborhood. Allow nature to become part of your vocabulary, and you're going to find that the human voice is only one source of stimulation, and not the most powerful one by any means.

If for good reasons you can't get out of the house or step away from your workplace, you can still experience nature up close.

I love books like *The Hidden Life of Trees*, *The Secret Life of the Owl*, *H Is for Hawk*, and *The Secret Life of Cows*. Yes, the authors of these books seem to create interior lives for creatures and things that may not be there, but at the very least I felt, and you may, too, a connection to the natural world based on keen and loving observations.

I've also found a bunch of videos on YouTube of thunderstorms and rain forests, and just fifteen or twenty minutes of a downpour with headphones on, and the atmosphere at home or work seems cleansed.

It's not anecdotal. Dr. Oliver Sacks, the noted neurologist and writer, wrote in his book *Everything in Its Place*, "Clearly, nature calls to something very deep in us. The role that nature plays in health and healing becomes even more critical for people working long days in windowless offices, for those living in city neighborhoods without access to green spaces, for children in city schools or for those in institutional settings such as nursing homes. The effects of nature's qualities on health are not only spiritual and emotional but physical and neurological."

Be part of nature, that's the goal, by forming attachments to big things, like the major seasons, and to small, incremental changes. If you are paying attention by the day, by the hour, to what goes on around you, you simply won't have as much time for things that make you miserable or drive you crazy. But don't worry! You'll still have time. You just won't have as *much* time.

*Chapter
Seven*

Silence

It's as if the entire nation of Japan has been read the Miranda warning: "You have the right to remain silent. Anything you say can be used against you in court. . . ."

Silence in Japan is part of the national character, and so essential to the culture that its uses and misuses define in large measure the ways in which people relate to one another both intimately and at work.

Silence as a cultural value in Japan goes back centuries. Check out the writing of Kenkō, whom I mentioned before: "Can you imagine a well-bred man talking with the authority of a know-it-all, even about a matter with which he is in fact familiar? The boor who pops up on the scene from somewhere in the hinterland answers questions with an air of utter authority in every field. . . . It is impressive when a man is always slow to speak, even on subjects he knows thoroughly, and does not speak at all unless questioned."

And yet, while silence, circumspection, nonverbal communication through posture and facial expression, and so on have benefits, there are drawbacks.

What if you say the wrong thing? What is the wrong thing? How do you know? What if you misread the mood? By misunderstanding the other person, you've been really disrespectful. Not only have you offended them, you've shown yourself to be so self-centered that you failed to recognize what others are thinking. You may not belong in this group. You should be ashamed of yourself.

Better to say nothing!

As a foreigner, an adult male from the West, I don't catch this vibe when I talk or do something that is alien to the culture. Oh, sure, if I were a rude person, or demanding, or the sort of individual who thinks his home is in the Greatest Country in the World, well, then, yeah, there would be problems.

But I'm not that guy.

My m.o. is to try to be like everyone else in a new place: to move like the people around me, to adopt their phrases, even to take on the tempo of their speech. I'm really passive in Japan; I try to let things happen and surrender to the situation, to whoever's in charge.

And, as I've said, my friends there have taught me a lot and continue to do so, starting many years ago.

This set of adaptive behaviors is observed by Japanese, of course, who often then find my efforts wildly amusing. The criticism they foist upon one another for not conforming to groups is not generally applied to me. As an outsider who behaves himself, or at least tries, sometimes clownishly, I get to observe and participate, and ironically because I'm not regarded as one of them, not being part of the group, I'm not expected to behave consistently like others *in* the group. (I have to be taught, tolerated, or ignored.)

At least, it's rare for anyone there to say something mean to me. I obey the rules: no talking on the train, no loud voices, shoes off on *tatami* mats, wash up before going in the hot springs, listen and observe instead of offering an opinion, don't ask a lot of questions, often say "please," "thank you," "excuse me," don't show a lot of emotion, sit still, and so on and so on and so on.

I especially love the silence and how it is used to communicate far more than words.*

We have a lot to learn from Japan about the *choice* to remain silent, especially when faced with adversity, and how it's a way to demonstrate acceptance. Silence can and ought to be a position taken to observe and listen and establish intimacy. Silence is also a way to establish social authority through restraint and self-control, a way to show you do not have to react to provocation, and a sign that you are thinking things through rather than relying on your emotions for decision making.

Trust me: I grew up in a family where emotion was the currency of exchange. Many nights back then, I'd rather have been broke.

---

*While silence in Japan is enormously helpful in developing trust, respecting others, learning through listening and observing, and accepting the world around and within you, it can also be a sign of fear, shame, sadness, and resignation. As I said at the beginning, let's cherry-pick the best of Japanese culture. We can avoid being silent when speaking up is called for, necessary, and the better alternative. Don't suffer in silence.

We have here the sounds of silence, silent nights, and silent lovemaking. *Choosing* to be silent is a whole lot different and better than *being* silenced. Silence is accompanied by a desire and effort to accept the other person's mood, to suss out that individual's thoughts and feelings, and to try to pay as much attention to their needs as you do to your own.

At its best, this kind of silence exemplifies Japanese relatedness and is a supreme form of acceptance. You're not judging or opining about others; you are silently empathizing with them, trying to feel what they feel and think what they think. It goes back to a definition of *ukeireru*: "Used by a mother with a child to accept something gently." A parent holds a child, the silence of their embrace.

When my son and daughter were tiny, there were times when holding them—not talking much, just feeling their warmth—was the best form of acceptance. Often on the three days each week when I was in charge, my wife left for work as the three of us nestled together while I held open a picture book, turning its pages for the zillionth time. And on the three days when I left for work, I would return home and often see the three of them silently coloring in the same place in the house where we had been that morning.

Then, too, when in nature, accepting the majesty of what you're seeing brings you closer to what's around you. If you're busy talking and offering your opinions, you can't take things in.

I work as a psychologist entirely with individuals from communities in which there is extensive urban poverty: Roxbury, Mattapan, Dorchester. Interviewing people to try to figure out who they appear to be, what shaped them, their resiliencies and terrors, the things that get in the way of their well-being and what sustains them. Much of what's happening between us is nonverbal. It's not that words fail us but rather that words don't come close to capturing what we have in common. We often don't share the same gender, race, education, economic class, age, or opportunities, so, as a result, we don't have the same words to describe our lives.

Words add to the nonverbal interaction but are not its focus. Words can also convey presumptions, judgments, and opinions, we all know, and misunderstandings show up like pickets in a fence. Better not to erect barriers, better at times to connect through nuanced gestures. We can try to relate to one another when we listen silently and observe posture and facial expression and tone of voice.

This is a well-known phenomenon, and it has been documented by psychologists, including Albert Mehrabian who wrote in his book *Nonverbal Communication* about the importance of tone of voice and facial expression as key to social interaction. Dr. Mehrabian summarized that "55% of communication is body language, 38% is the tone of voice, and 7% is the actual words spoken." Well, maybe, and not all the time, and depends on who you are with, and the situation, but it's hard to disagree with the core belief that a lot goes on between people that's unspoken.

In Japan, it can be considered rude to have to resort to words to communicate desires or concerns. You, the listener, are supposed to feel and think so much of what others feel and think that words aren't necessary. For others to have to verbalize what they are thinking or feeling is a sign that you aren't listening to them and that you fail to accept who they are. *Aun no kokyu*, as Yamakuse put it, "breathing in harmony."

The unspoken nature of social interaction creates hidden worlds. The relationships between friends and lovers have pockets that only they can see and feel. These are established and protected by silence. As Jun'ichirō Tanizaki, the great Japanese novelist, notes in his wonderful essay "In Praise of Shadows," "We find beauty not in the thing itself but in the pattern of shadows, the light and the darkness, that one thing against another creates."

I've experienced this countless times in Japan, the pleasure of things adumbrated, and the feeling while it's happening is so deep that it lasts years. You lose some awareness of yourself while accepting the other person, and that loss is liberating. You also have to focus on what the other person is trying to say without having to say it. That requires enormous concentration, which becomes part of the relationship. You wind up thinking a lot about others and less about yourself.

A lot of what I am unhappy about or afraid of or disappointed in is due to an unrealistic outlook developed through selfishness. I have a fantasy or idea, a set of expectations, related to my needs and my perceptions. These often have little or nothing to do with the other person who is causing me pain. As soon as I realized that it was my fantasies, ideas, and expectations that needed to change—rather than the other person—I felt a state of unfamiliar relaxation that I try to bring about as much as possible in relationships.

It's an awareness that my selfishness is what brings about the pain, rather than the other person. I find that just enjoying the intimacy of silence with another human being is often enough. After all, how many people do we have in our lives with whom we can sit in silence, whose company we enjoy so much that words aren't necessary?

The same applies to being in public. Many of us have been seated on planes beside people who tell us their life story before we reach cruising altitude. No disrespect, but . . .

Something else happens in Japan. When people get together, either in work settings or on social occasions, questions are not asked in a flurry. I've discovered this when working in Japan and interviewing all sorts of people.

Ask one question.

Wait for the answer.

Don't interrupt.

Don't offer an opinion.

Don't agree or disagree.

Don't share an experience from your own life that is similar to that of the person speaking.

Just listen.

Wait.

Sitting in silence creates the opportunity to see the situation from the other person's perspective. As a result, the mood between you and the other person, how you feel while observing, becomes a focal point. You both have goals in mind, but way before you can get to these, you are establishing silent acceptance of one another. That type of acceptance can make the achievement of the goal inevitable rather than a struggle.

It's more important that the two of you are understood and respected than that one of you achieves more power. Which is what silence offers at its zenith: respect for those around you.

Whether you are on a busy sidewalk in Nihonbashi or a crowded restaurant, noise levels are at a minimum. It's impossible to eavesdrop on whispered conversations. There are hardly any street musicians. No yelling into cell phones. No greetings exchanged by shouts between friends.

Respect is conveyed through gestures. A group of business people bowing to one another after a successful meeting. A chef outside his restaurant waving goodbye to customers until they are no longer in view. You don't see a lot of hugging or kissing, nor do many hold hands, but affection is evident in the simultaneity of steps taken by a young couple who might be in love.

To the extent that there are any loud noises, these come from the pounding clang of metal ball bearings from inside colorful gambling machines of pachinko parlors. Blaring bullhorns on small trucks of political candidates shouting that Japan will rise again. Speakers attached to doorways of discount stores: *Bargains! Sales! Specials!* Even inside the massive, chaotic Shinjuku train station in Tokyo, where over a million commuters pass through each day, the sound is of footsteps, high heels and black, laced shoes, people running to catch a train, rather than of loud voices.

Individuals are diminished in all of this. The surroundings swallow them up. Who you are matters less than where you are, and your opinions don't matter as much as the environment. Unlike an American city, in which what you say defines in part where you are, the urban environment in Japan is definitive. Being respectful means being part of your surroundings, not using your voice to differentiate or separate yourself. This has a calming, inclusive effect.

Japanese cope with pressure through demonstrations of respect. OK, don't get in the way of a salaryman who's late for his meeting as he dashes for the train. And keep your hands to yourself. But respect for others is evident in Japan among friends and colleagues and strangers more often than not, and these silent, physical displays are central to civic life.

It's a way to show acceptance of others. The quiet creates unity and is a coherent and widespread effort to make sure that whatever is on your mind doesn't interfere with someone else. Since Japanese participate in this unspoken way of life, groups form in which one is accepted, more or less, and assumed to share similar thoughts and feelings.

It's understood that this isn't always the case. Japanese culture is anything but naive—the emotional sophistication is like advanced calculus. But why talk and act in ways that are potentially divisive to group norms? That's part of why what isn't said in Japan is often more important than what *is* said.

The demonstrations of respect are meaningful. Empathy is conveyed. It does not matter (for the moment) if you agree or disagree with what or who is around you. What matters is silent acceptance: what or who is around you has a right to be there, and that right is guaranteed and safeguarded by your show of respect.

Applying respect, empathy, and acceptance to the world around you starts with how you feel and think about yourself. If you're miserable, afraid, and angry, good luck being respectful to others.

One way to rid yourself of self-loathing is to change the conditions around you. The effort is worth it. By accepting what and who are around you, you have a chance to create a better environment that, in turn, can shape who you are and how you feel about yourself. That kind of acceptance is a very subtle and effective way of making personal change.

Japan falls short of acceptance in workplaces and communities. But in everyday life, the rules of social discourse, the typical ways in which people at home and in public treat one another, are a valuable guide to how we might adapt that kind of respect to our versatile and vibrant lives here.

Again, I am thinking of a combination of American *and* Japanese cultures, a recognition that the whole is greater than the sum of the parts. Applying the respectful behaviors of Japan to our lives, to the bedrock here of spontaneity and diversity of thought, suggests possibilities.

Which is why showing respect for others is not only empathic but a way to reduce *internal* stress. By moving through life accepting adversity through respect for others and the situation, you can establish a foundation for yourself that at the very least preserves your dignity. And that effort toward dignity is what respect in Japan is all about.

People in life will shove you and be impolite, but that doesn't mean you have to respond in kind. And by showing your best face to the world, it's a signal that you expect others to treat you with respect. Look, I know it doesn't always work, and, yes, our emotions often get the better of us, but acting respectful through silent behaviors can reframe any number of situations.

Japanese show respect daily in numerous ways.

Bowing takes place in public and in private. Sometimes a sign of obeisance is a deep bow to a person who responds with a slight bow, but often the bows more or less match up.

Returning from Japan, I find myself leaning forward a little, tilting my head, and straightening my shoulders. It feels good to use my posture to convey respect. I like the sensation of averting my eyes, too, I'm not sure why.

Just to be clear: bowing is not about giving in, surrendering authority, or conveying inferiority. This is not about deference. On the contrary: bowing, like the Western handshake, is a simplification of relatedness. Two people bow to one another to convey mutual respect. And, yes, there are numerous instances of an employee bowing way deeper to the boss than the boss bows to the employee, but that signifies a relationship that exists outside of the bowing. It's essential, at a minimum, to recognize Japanese culture as meaningful independent of Western values. That, too, is another way of showing respect.

And, sure, you may not want to bow—it's definitely goofy if you're a Westerner going full tilt—but you *can* use your body to show acceptance. Having a relaxed posture, strolling rather than strutting, loosening up—all send a sign to others that you don't want to dominate the room. In turn, if you're lucky, people might relax their postures, too.

Expression of respect among Japanese takes place with acute awareness of others.

At a sumo match in Tokyo, I lounged with friends and ate *yakitori* and drank beer while the enormous wrestlers fought in the ring below. Most spectators were quietly riveted until a wrestler was shoved out of the ring or thrown down. Then the applause and cheering were deafening.

When I took my friend Nozomi to a Boston Celtics basketball game, and he didn't say a word throughout the game, I suggested we leave early. I thought he wasn't having a good time. But he looked surprised and asked to stay, so we remained in our seats until the final buzzer. On the subway home, he didn't stop talking about the game—he remembered a lot of the plays and scoring baskets, he had absorbed what he had seen, and his respect for the event enabled him to observe it.

At Japanese baseball games, the crowd often cheers madly, almost from beginning to end, until you feel as if you're part of something, you've joined in, you are no longer an individual, you are part of the group. It's an extreme version of being a sports fan in the United States—there are set cheers and chants and rituals. When I went to a game with my daughter, I saw the fans of the Tokyo Yakult Swallows raise umbrellas and open and close them repeatedly every time one of their players scored a home run.

Jazz, too.

At a performance inside Cotton Club, which is located in the Marunouchi district of Tokyo, no one touched their drinks, whispered, or moved very much while the band performed. The key was both to absorb the music and to allow others to do the same. It was reverential.

Respect creates conditions necessary for observation. When you have awareness of your surroundings, and what these surroundings expect of you, you are better able to accept the situation. This is not only true for a daily routine and public entertainment, but it applies to stressful situations.

A few years back, Delta landed us at Narita Airport, just outside of Tokyo, knowing (but not telling passengers) that all public and private transportation had been shut down and that no rooms were available for fifty miles. (The plane had landed in Nagoya to refuel, but no one was allowed off because, Delta explained to me later, they did not want to be asked to pay for hotel rooms.) After about thirteen hours in the air, I joined hundreds of Japanese sleeping on the floor of the airport, and it wasn't until sixteen hours later that trains were running. I'm not saying we all adopted a Zen-like approach, but what did happen was a valuable lesson.

It got very quiet. People curled up on coats near one another. It was not resignation nor hopelessness, but an understanding that showing anger would make things worse for everyone, that there was nothing any of us could do to change the situation, and that perhaps, best of all, we might, each one of us, show calm and restraint. It would have been considered selfish and disrespectful to show anger. Being silent and peaceful was a recognition that what was happening was not about each one of us but about all of us, recognizing that respect for the well-being of others was more important than individual stress.

I've taken that mentality into other situations far removed from the day and night at Narita. It boils down to something very much a part of Japanese psychology: the situation may be stressful, but it does not mean that I have to respond to it stressfully.

I can respect the turmoil, I can even accept it, but I refuse to be part of it, and I refuse to allow it to have bearing upon who I am as a person. I can choose to ignore it; I do not have to react.*

This approach requires enormous effort, and if you have seen me driving in Boston, cutting off a driver on an exit ramp, you will know that it remains an ideal worth striving for.

The idea is to build a respectful community of which you are a part, where your needs are understood in the context of others. There are always people who are weaker than you and who need your help. Acting based on your community means tempering your reactions and behavior based on needs other than yours.

These concepts of respect, silence, and acceptance have an impact on major issues in Japan: end-of-life care and

---

*Except, of course, to write about it years later, and never to fly Delta again. But angry? I'm not angry. Who said anything about being angry?

palliation (the biggest medical costs occur usually in the last six months of a person's life); access to medical care for those who are healthy; ongoing care for those with chronic disorders; and safe urban centers.

If you chiefly care for yourself and your family, and let others fend for themselves, that's not respect; that's a business plan.

Japanese recognize that how we feel about ourselves is affected by how others live around us. It's worth the personal sacrifice in order to create environments that are respectful.

Respect for others is a way to show self-respect. Respect for how you fall short of your ideals, your failures, and, in general, the ways in which you have made a mess of things. (I'm talking about myself here, in case you're wondering.) Respect for yourself builds self-confidence.

With that in mind: bow a little, show patience, accept that others are stressed out, observe silently, and listen.

The zero-sum game that typifies so many exchanges in the West is put aside. There often isn't a clear winner or loser. Both parties feel good about the exchange, and it is chiefly through silence that this has been established. With a *choice* to be silent and respectful come benefits. Best of all, you gain strength for times when speaking up is necessary.

Chapter Eight

Apologies

Sumimasen was the first word I learned in Japan. I heard the word spoken everywhere, I heard it said a lot. In stores, in train stations, on the street, in elevators, at business meetings, in restaurants and bars and cafés, and in all sorts of situations.

I would hold open a door for someone.

"*Sumimasen*," that person would say.

Out with friends, eating *tonkatsu*, Kanna puts up her hand to signal the waiter and says: "*Sumimasen.*"

A phone conversation: the speaker is bowing to the person on the other end of the line, who can't see his show of deference, and he repeats the word each time he inclines his head: "*Sumimasen. Sumimasen. Sumimasen.*" (He interjects, "*Sumimasen*," with a declaration of "*Hai!*," which means "*Yes!*" and implies "*Yes, will do!*" or "*Yes, understood!*")

When years ago on my first visit I asked friends what *sumimasen* means, I was told that it's a rough approximation of "I'm sorry" and a form of an apology. But why would you apologize to a waiter? And why say it a bunch of times on the phone? Or when someone holds the door open for

131

you? No, *sumimasen* is a lot more complicated than just "I'm sorry," and although it can be understood and applied to our lives here, the word, like many expressions and behaviors in Japan, has several meanings that depend on when, where, and to whom it is said. I learned that from the same friends.

What we're talking about is respect and acceptance for other human beings by apologizing for taking them away from what they are doing or saying. *Sumimasen* requires the other person to whom you are saying it to acknowledge your existence and by doing so alters what they are doing. It's a way to say: I'm sorry for inconveniencing you. I'm sorry that you have to deal with me and my needs. I'm sorry for being selfish.

There can also be a hint of being ironic when it's said, but there is irony in much of what we say because how often do we express what we're *really* thinking rather than adapt to the demands of what any given situation calls for?

Irony is part of the ubiquitous apology in Japanese life.

When the novelist Tanizaki praises shadows, he is saying that what you see, what you take for real, isn't as real as what goes on behind the curtain. In a culture as visual as Japan, so much of what is observable is an ironic representation of meaning rather than the thing itself. Which leaves a lot of what *is* seen open to interpretation.

But *sumimasen* is *also* a sincere attempt to see and accept a situation from another person's point of view. It takes what you feel and think into the realm of someone else's experience.

This mix of sincerity and irony isn't as abstract as it might sound. As Roland Barthes noted in *Empire of Signs*, "the rational is merely one system among others," and "the whole of Zen wages a war against the prevarication of meaning." If you accept that the unseen or the unconscious or the irrational are a big part of what create meaning in our lives, you understand some of what makes up Japanese culture. Namely, what we see and say is a *representation* or a sign of deep meaning.

The deeper meaning of *sumimasen* is that both the person saying it as well as the person to whom it is said now have an apology instead of the anger or frustration or request or inconvenience that prompted the apology in the first place.

Rather than facing a divisive conflict or disruption, both people have something in common. They accept that the situation is difficult; the apology takes a potentially static circumstance and changes it. *Sumimasen* has the potential, in fact, to change *everything*.

The person saying, "*Sumimasen*," accepts that what prompted the apology may have been difficult for the person causing the problem. Maybe that person was having a bad day. Or is following a script provided by a company. Or simply doesn't care.

Whatever it is, *your* apology is a way to accept the situation and to give the person who appears to have caused it an opportunity to change and make things better. If the person to whom one is apologizing uses your *sumimasen* to make things worse, that's, as one often hears in Japan, a misunderstanding.

"Ah, sorry for the misunderstanding!" But at least the person saying, "*Sumimasen*," tried!

Having witnessed and experienced the positive impact that saying *sumimasen* has in Japan, I apologize here all the time and every day, in all sorts of situations. It has an effect that's wonderful to observe as well as being useful in making everyone feel less stressed out.

When speaking with the phone company about a technical glitch, or the city about a parking ticket I *know* was unfair, I start the conversation by saying something along the lines of: "I'm sorry, I apologize for taking your time, and I appreciate your help. I wonder if . . ."

"Oh, no need to apologize" is often the response, or among younger people, "No worries."

Dude, I wasn't worried.

I can hear surprise in the person's voice, and that element of surprise is the sign of a fresh start, the possibility that the person on the other end of the line isn't going to put up a wall. Not right away. Maybe that person will actually listen to what I have to say, see that since it feels good talking to someone who isn't angry it may be worthwhile to try to be helpful.

Even if I lose out and my concern is dismissed, at least I've avoided being angry, which enables me to stay relatively focused for the rest of the day. As we all know, anger is a huge distraction. It's not even properly speaking an emotion in the sense that it doesn't come from within us but is instead a reaction to what's going on around us. By not reacting, we have a shot at staying calm. And staying calm, we can get things done.

For sure, this isn't what people in customer service or retail positions are accustomed to hearing from disgruntled customers. They gear up for a fight; they're sure that you are going to insult them, make some weird demand, ask to speak to their supervisor, and so on. So you really have an advantage when instead of flipping out, you smile and say with sincerity, "I apologize. I wonder if you can help me."

You have to be sincere. This isn't a strategy or tactic. You have to *feel* it. It's unexpected, being pleasant and apologetic, and at the moment of surprise, you pounce!

Wait, did I just write that? *Pounce*?!

Oh, *sumimasen*, I didn't mean to write *pounce*. I meant to write that you can establish a degree of affiliation so that the person to whom you are apologizing relates to you. Your apology makes them happy. You've made them happy! Let's hope that they will then want to be of help to the person who made them happy rather than angry, scared, and defensive.

For those of you in customer service who are reading this and have to deal with angry, rude, entitled customers who want what they want when they want it, who haven't yet read this helpful book, start the conversation with: "Sorry that we have to start this way. I'm sorry that we have this difficulty."

And in far more important and consequential situations, at work with colleagues or people waiting to be seen or bosses, saying, "I'm sorry," goes a long way to defusing stress.

And with a spouse or lover or friend, apologizing—even if you're convinced you've done little or nothing wrong—means that you're accepting the other person's point of view. It makes their anger or frustration legit—and, trust me, that works.

No, not all the time. But *when* it works, you have gained authority over your emotions and recognized that what matters to you matters less than what matters to the person you love or care about.

Sumimasen is an effort to avoid or resolve conflict, which is something Japanese are exceedingly good at doing *within their culture*. When the focus is on the group or relationship, and not the individual, conflicts are not seen primarily as individual problems but as insults to a well-established group mentality. When you apologize, you are acknowledging that the group, even if it's only two of you, matters more than you. It's an empathic approach.

Yes, I'll get sly looks, on occasion, as if I have something up my sleeve. The checkout person at Target is not used to a customer apologizing to him for *his* fogging out. (If he bothered to stop texting, he might, in fact, get the line going and out the door.) Nor is the DMV employee accustomed to someone apologizing when asking for a sticker to put on the license plate that should have been sent in the mail but wasn't, and that the result was a $50 ticket.

But what's the point in being yet another predictable, angry customer when you can say, "I'm sorry"? And why continue to try to defend yourself with people at work or attempt to win arguments at home? An apology can lead to a discussion rather than a fight. As in: "I'm sorry we're arguing about this. I apologize for making things worse."

Maybe that's why *sumimasen* is often said repeatedly by speakers in Japan. The first time might be misconstrued as a trick or strategy, but by the second or third time it's said, the listener gets it: You're sorry! You really are sorry.

You have the authority to change the situation, you have the power to make things better. You're not following a script; you're not on the PA lying through your teeth about why the train is delayed; you're not yelling at your spouse. No, you're the one saying, "I'm sorry." That's the secret behind *sumimasen*. The apology is for the person making it, not the person receiving it.

You'll feel better after apologizing even if the person who's hearing you say it doesn't. It's a relief not to react to a stressful situation. You can apologize for being part of the problem, for contributing to the awful situation, for not caring enough to tamp things down. You're accepting responsibility for your disruptive behavior.

An apology means that you accept things as they are but not that you are resigned to things staying that way. Maybe without the anger, it will be possible to care enough to do something so that in the future it won't be necessary to say, "*Sumimasen.*"

Chapter Nine

Everything Is Nothing

Jiro told me I had to leave.

We were on the top floor of a tall government building in Kanazawa. We were there to try to get funding from the prefecture for a project we hoped to do together—a booklet about the artisans of the Yamanaka region who provide work to his *ryokan*. Jiro was in charge of the artisans, and I was to do the writing.

My teenage son, Nick, was waiting downstairs in the cavernous lobby, which vaulted straight up about twelve floors and was bordered within by long, open corridors. You could hear the echo of shoes from down below, and often it was the sound of people running. The lobby's windows were a couple of stories high. You could see out, though there wasn't much to see: a big lot of shiny parked cars, dutifully washed and looking brand new, in the distance facing east low mountains, a two-lane road with a 7-Eleven and a brightly colored diner.

"Yes," Jiro whispered, "we have business to discuss, administrative matters, and it is preferable that you join us afterwards."

Jiro had warned me in advance, and his directive and my response, "Yes, I understand," were pretty much scripted and understood as such by the prefectural official.

Because I had known this would happen, I had done a little research about what to see and do while discussions from which I was excluded were held.

The D. T. Suzuki Museum was close by. Suzuki is credited with popularizing Zen Buddhism in the West. I had read some of his books.* I had told Jiro I would like to visit the museum, and he had instructed his driver to take us there. The museum was designed by the architect Yoshio Taniguchi, who also redesigned the Museum of Modern Art (MOMA) in New York City. Dana Buntrock, the eminent scholar of Japanese architecture, described Taniguchi as "the master of minimalism," and his confidence in what is not there, what is implied, is evident in his work.

Nick and I were unaware of Taniguchi's reputation, and neither of us are architecture scholars, so it was all the more impressive that we felt what we felt. We experienced the museum without being analytical or informed—that would come later. For the time being, while we were inside Taniguchi's creation, we might be able to sense what he had wanted us to sense. We were there because of Suzuki, not the buildings which housed his work.

We entered through an unremarkable doorway and then took a few steps to a glassed-in ticket counter. After pur-

---

*D. T. Suzuki (1870–1966) was a Japanese writer and philosopher who was married to Beatrice Erskine Lane, an American philosopher.

chasing tickets, we were handed a small brochure that contained a map to guide us through the museum. We walked through the rooms, soothed by our thoughts, and looked at manuscripts and photographs in display cases and on walls, arranged chronologically so we passed through Suzuki's life, and with a sparseness that deepened our appreciation.

We reached an area just outside of the museum's main building, the Contemplative Space and Water Mirror Garden, and here felt something strange and deeper. The space is a dark, square room, with openings on all its sides and views of a garden. There is nothing to see in the room. The emptiness is the truest thing about the space. You sit on wide wooden platforms and look up and out in silence.

We sat a long time, and it wasn't until much later that Nick told me that this was the most beautiful museum he had ever visited. He had been to a lot of museums, and I wasn't sure what it was that he loved most about this one. He talked about emptiness. Going into a place where nothing is there and feeling that everything is there inspires well-being.

Neither of us were fooled by the apparent lack of artifice: those long, slender lines, the granite, the amount of light allowed in, the texture of the floor and platforms were all remarkable and evocative. Nothing there, but, oh, what nothing!

When the car picked us up and brought us back to Jiro, he could see from our faces that we were really happy. We didn't have to say anything.

He said, "I'm so glad you enjoyed the museum."

His *ryokan* makes great use of the silence and emptiness that we had experienced at the Suzuki Museum. Nothing on its walls. Bare spaces. The forest and courtyard garden are visible from nearly everywhere within the interior. No need or desire to distract. No need or desire to inform. Just a way to accept that we are close to nothing, and that nothingness informs our brief presence on earth.

Nearby is another *ryokan*, Beniya Mukayu, where the name itself is a sign of the outlook that informs Japanese use of space. Sachiko Nakamichi, who owns the property with her husband, Kazunari, told me that *mukayu* means, more or less, "everything is nothing." What you experience here, too, are bare walls and silence.

Years spent visiting Japan changed my outlook on how I use space back home in the States. Like many people, I had tended to hold on to things, stretching back years, and while there is little or no utility or purpose to these things, I found it hard to let go.*

How could I throw out my Clash T-shirt from 1981? That was the summer I saw them perform three times, once in a mosh pit in Asbury Park with my ex-girlfriend's kid sister, Mary. If I threw that out, it would be like throwing out a part of myself, right?

My study was filled, floor to ceiling, with clippings from newspapers and magazines of important world events, articles

---

*If you are thinking about Marie Kondo, *sumimasen*. Just hold on to your broom for a few minutes.

I'd written while in college, books I would never read. Hats, shoes, small appliances, knickknacks, and souvenirs. Each one had a memory that I could call up.

Like the little clay hippie figurine holding a sign: "Fight Hate." My mom and I had gone to a home where a woman and her son were selling what we used to call "novelty items," which my mom wanted to pick up as party favors. The son wore a dress and makeup, something I'd never seen a man do before, and that afternoon is indelible.

Or the little red tin that had held cigars from a trip I had made with my dad to Holland ages ago. He had rented a car, handed me a map, and put me in charge of getting around. He didn't care where we went as long as we could find a small hotel with rooms available by midafternoon.

If I got rid of these things, would I forget who I had been and the people who had been there with me?

Well, maybe so. Could be that's the point. Letting go of things might be a healthy decision. Move on. Then I could better attach myself to the present. Reminders that prompt memories get in the way of accepting the present.

What was I afraid of *now*? Why look back?

Don't look back.

I also thought about what I want and what I would do to get it. What would I give up to get more? What demands would I place on myself, what demands would I obey, in order to acquire more stuff? How much stuff did I need?

How do you know when you have *enough stuff*?

The more I thought about it, the more I realized I wanted less, and I was happier not just with less, but with not wanting more. That's not a realization that came overnight. It took, oh, let's say, the better part of a decade, but once I accepted it as true, it led to change.

I went to Staples and bought a half dozen big, clear plastic containers, and dumped all sorts of detritus into them, and stored it all in the cellar *for now*. I promise to get rid of it one day. I promise!

A little bust of Abraham Lincoln, my schoolboy world globe, countless index cards with indecipherable writing, and so on. But I also threw out lots of stuff. I would say I threw out about four times more things than what I kept. I let go.

I felt cleansed. I felt like a free human being. I felt better able to accept loss as necessary in order to acquire well-being.

My study, following this cleansing, was nearly empty. A tall desk typically used by architectural draftspeople, a tall chair, a comfortable chair for reading, two lamps that are usually used in photography studios, an original movie poster in Japanese of *High and Low*, the birth announcements of my two children, a map of the Tokyo subway system, and, OK, piles of books.

Most everything was gone. It wasn't quite a "contemplative space," but it was the emptiest room I'd ever made for myself.

Now a few words about cleaning up. I swear, and I imagine you won't believe me, but I had not heard of Marie Kondo until after I showed this chapter to a friend and she pointed out that, um, Marie was there long before me and most of us seeking to get rid of clutter. So all credit to Ms. Kondo and her book *The Life-Changing Magic of Tidying Up*. Nothing but respect.[*]

Those of us in the worldwide Clean-Up Crew[†] agree: There are great benefits, psychologically and emotionally, to emptying out our rooms. What else might change as a result of living in the present with fewer reminders of the past?

Did I really need a new iPhone with every iteration? Why buy more clothing? Why buy more *anything*?

This business of having more raises questions about risks and benefits. What are the benefits of having more? What are the risks? Maybe it's preferable to enjoy what you have rather than acquire more in order to try to feel better. How much better can you feel? How much do you lose of yourself while trying to get more in order to feel better about yourself?

Free of most things in my study, I discovered that it wasn't that I was losing my past. On the contrary, now the past was in me; now the past was unseen; now I was the past. It was a great way of accepting change.

---

[*] A BBC report notes: "Kondo is far from the only one advocating this simpler, tidier lifestyle. In the UK, Sophie Hinchliffe, better known as Mrs. Hinch, has been demonstrating to her Instagram followers and TV viewers how having a cleaner, tidier home can lead to a better life, while in California, professional organizer Beth Penn has written a book and set up her own company to help people sort out their stuff. There are dozens of other books and decluttering services to be found with a quick search of the internet." When our surroundings feel full, it can also make us feel more anxious and stressed, with one study by psychologists Rena Repetti and Darby Saxby at UCLA finding mothers living in messy houses had higher levels of the stress hormone cortisol.

[†] The first rule of Clean-Up Crew is there is no Clean-Up Crew.

Arata Isozaki, the 2019 winner of the Pritzker Architecture Prize, may have said it best: "Like the universe, architecture comes out of nothing, becomes something, and eventually becomes nothing again. That life cycle from birth to death is a process that I want to showcase." His words apply to life outside of his field, and his eighty-seven years inform his observations. These observations are about acceptance of loss and temporality while at the same time an invitation to participate and contribute to the world.

Taking inspiration from this master architect, it's possible to envision ways to express observing what's around me rather than imposing my particularities. The nothingness is a sign that one day I'll disappear, too. Recognizing and using that awareness of a void shows acceptance rather than resistance to or denial of this natural inevitability. When Isozaki refers to birth and death, he is implying a kind of renewal.

Why pretend otherwise by filling up rooms with detritus? Why deny death through accumulation? All that stuff implies you're going to be around to enjoy it for a long time, but in fact you're here today and . . .

*Chapter
Ten*

No Place Is Ever
Quite Like Home

When I was invited into a Japanese home for the first time, I saw after removing my shoes and putting on house slippers, then stepping up to a foyer leading into the living room, a small wooden cabinet to my right that held black-and-white headshots of people I took to be deceased family members. Along with the photos was an array of what appeared to be religious objects.

My host told me that what I was looking at was a *butsudan*, and then he explained further, before we sat and had tea and sweets that his grandmother brought out while showing us a book filled with calligraphy and stamped by monks from temples she had visited with her husband many years earlier.

Her husband was, of course, one of the men in the photos.

Butsudan appear to be little cabinets, or shelves, and are often stationed in the foyers of homes, positioned as watchtowers. *Butsudan* are sort of like an altar or a reliquary, housing Buddhist icons and *butsugu*, which are containers for incense, fruit, and so on. Physical reminders of the spirituality that informs our lives, *butsudan* take on many meanings, depending on the home and the people who are honoring the past.

Butsudan appear in Japanese homes to remind the living that their thoughts and actions are being judged, observed, and accepted by their ancestors.

Well, not exactly.

These shrines are a means of *honoring* the dead and *accepting* their loss, but when you cut to the chase, isn't the message that you should think and behave in ways the dead expect of you? If you act in ways you imagine would disappoint the dead, you are dishonoring them. This makes for good behavior but could be a straitjacket.

Or maybe it's neither. Because who knows what the dead expect of you? They're gone; you're still here.

Butsudan can sanction your actions. You can say to yourself, "Oh, I'm just the sort of person my grandfather wants me to be!" knowing that he'll never know.

Your behavior is up to you—you're responsible for your actions, what you think and do—and the idea that your ancestors are watching over you, sanctioning or condemning your behavior is really creative and useful *fiction*.

It provides a context for your life: people who love you are watching over you, and through your actions you are keeping them alive, in a way, and carrying them forward into the future.

Our lives are the sum of the stories of our families. *Butsudan* are physical reminders of the family stories that make us who we are.

By saying *spirituality*, I mean the unseen, the unknown, and the inexplicable that guide and distract and preoccupy each of us, leading us to act in ways regrettable, sudden, erotic— ways that take us by surprise. Japanese culture is pulled toward darkness and shadows, to an acceptance of what nature has in store for us, of what nature expects of us, of how we might see ourselves through the eyes of our ancestors, which is an imaginative leap.

The very cool thing about *butsudan* is that, to paraphrase Maurice Sendak, you're in the ancestors and the ancestors are in you. How you imagine their acceptance is in your head, and *butsudan* are physical reminders that yes, you're right, whatever you do, your ancestors *might* approve.

It's not quite as easy as that. A *butsudan* is not a "Get Out of Jail Free" card. If you have a *butsudan* and allow it to influence your thoughts, emotions, awareness, relationships, and decision making, you are genuinely bringing ancestors into your life as meaningful context. After all, it is a literal, physical reminder that the past is present always.

Even if the construct of ancestors is fictional, in the sense that you are the ancestor being imagined, you now have a historical conscience or tradition in which your behavior is taking place. You are no longer operating entirely in the present or in anticipation of the future, not precisely considering your legacy, but adding to all these, you have the sense that you are part of a family stretching deep into the unseen and unknown past.

In accepting their loss, you are deepening your awareness of the world, acting in accordance with the past.

If you behave atrociously, you are not only unpleasant to those around you but showing disrespect to those who are responsible for your existence. *Butsudan* are a way to accept loss and transform it into ongoing acts of respect.

The catch is that previous generations were not exactly batting a thousand. All of us have to try to be better. I don't mean loyalty, bravery, resilience, or patience. Previous generations nailed those values, in many ways, and their examples continue to serve as signposts for us.

But when it comes to race, gender, and class, they usually come up empty-handed.

The task is to take a look at the *butsudan* and be inspired by the extraordinary depth of our ancestors' courage while recognizing that we can apply their positive values to today's stressful concerns.

In considering *butsudan*, we have the opportunity to add meaning to our lives. Not just to think about our happiness or need for stability, but of others who preceded us. And in accepting their loss, in making them part of our lives, to consider: *What would my grandfather do?* What we do reflects on our family.

Having ancestors in your home can be a haunting experience, fraught with anxiety, and it can be a source of well-being. Their presence means that there is bound to be vacillation. Some days Grandpa will approve. Other days, not so much. It's really up to you to behave in ways that you *imagine* will invite approval. The wonder of it all is that the *butsudan* is a *physical* prompt to make use of your imagination.

The point of *butsudan* isn't to celebrate the past with all its pitfalls and disappointments. Truth be told, the past is always in our heads; our prior experiences dictate our behaviors, awareness, and decision making, like it or not.

This may not bear mentioning, but just in case, let's agree that the past—good and bad, evil and whatnot—is a big part of the unconscious and at times conscious control panel of our lives.

Butsudan create an idealized, physical version of ancestors, perhaps, or, at the very least, ancestors who are no longer just imagined authorities but can be seen by the person in whose home the *butsudan* is placed.

Butsudan are not literal but representational, similar to what Roland Barthes notes in his work: a sign; interpret it as you can or like. Once the past is physical, not just in our heads, that representation or sign has the potential to be re-interpreted perhaps more readily by the living.

You can buy yourself a *butsudan* from any number of outfits on the Internet and stack the shelves and fill the interior with photographs, incense, and oranges.*

(This isn't clutter. This is a tiny shrine.)

Another option is to rely upon your own complex culture, assuming you are not Japanese, and set up a shrine in your home to reflect your traditions. I've been in homes, most of us have, in which a wall in the kitchen is devoted to photos

---

*Nakayama is one such source: nakayamabutsudans.com.

of dozens of parents, grandparents, aunts and uncles, and cousins, some in formal poses, others at the beach, there to remind the people who live there that traditions are kept alive and inform us long after loved ones are gone.

Either way, the idea is that what you do can bring shame or glory, or lots in between, with variations each day, to your ancestors and to you as an extension of them.

I'm not someone who has faith in icons or images. There are few photographs of family in my home, and no *butsudan*. But for sure I think daily about my parents and grandparents, I'm troubled by loss, and I try each day to figure out how what I do is related to what they did.

It's a process of forgetting individualism, placing behavior into the realm of how my lost family might accept me.

There's a lot to be said for this peculiar forgetting of self through remembering others. It makes for a very intimate home. It downplays the momentousness of everyday stress. It's a reminder that we're not here for very long and that our significance derives in large measure from who came before us rather than what we are faced with now.

Look around your home and identify the objects that you have placed there to remind you of the people who are no longer in your life but who at times feel more real than colleagues at work, neighbors, and faces in the news.

Butsudan are a way of documenting history, in showing us that by accepting loss, we recreate (and embody) those we've lost, similar to what Hilary Mantel wrote, "What is to be done with the lost, the dead, but write them into being?"

Chapter
Eleven

Yes, I Understand

*H*ai and *wakarimashita* are the second and third words, after *sumimasen,* that I learned in Japan. I heard them said everywhere.

Declared into mouthpieces of phones cupped by speakers as they bent forward while bowing. Each face varied, but in common there appeared an earnest and purposeful look, an attentiveness and focused gaze, as if few things mattered more than the words being said.

"*Hai!*" Pause. "*Hai! Hai, wakarimashita! Hai!*"

Slight bow, phone put away, on with the rest of the day.

In restaurants, hotels, bars, cafés, shops, places of business, offices, and markets, eyes are averted, the direct eye-to-eye contact we value so much in the West is replaced largely by posture, tone of voice, tilt of head, and flow of speech. Your whole body, top to bottom, employing your senses, is used to convey meaning, respect, acceptance, and understanding of the other person.

Hai is a lot like saying yes and not at all like saying yes, which is a conundrum that leads to misunderstandings between Westerners and Japanese. The addition of the word *wakarimashita* after saying *hai* helps clear things up a little. It means "understood."

When Japanese say, "*Hai, wakarimashita,*" they may or may not be agreeing with you. It means that the person is saying that they understand what you said. This understanding creates a context for any decision that might follow what's *been* said.

How can I agree or disagree with you if we haven't even made clear if I understand exactly what it is you want me to do or what you expect of me? We haven't figured out our relationship to one another. "*Hai, wakarimashita*" is a way to establish relatedness.

Once that's been advanced, we can move toward possible resolution. I might do what you ask; I might not. You might hear irony in my *hai*, so that the next time we speak, you'll up the ante and ask, "*When* are you getting done what I asked you to do?" Or, "I want this done *by Friday.*" *Hai* is the preface to smooth implementation of plans.

I love many things about this process of negotiation and have applied it as an approach in situations with surprising and positive results.

It means trying hard—really, really hard—to be agreeable, not to frame things that could lead to escalation, and to be aware of why the other person might be provocative.

Recently I had to deal with a person who had hired me to do some writing in New York, and months went by without the necessary schedule of appointments. I lost sleep, I fought frustration and anger, and then it finally hit me: This person just didn't care. Not only about our project but about a lot of things. That realization helped me to see the problem that was created as a challenge in his overall life: I was just being made part of his generally not caring. Then I realized that a person who doesn't care is kind of a miserable human being. Overall, I was able to look at the situation as if I wasn't part of it.

Hai, wakarimashita, I thought. I understood. Knowing that he didn't care made our negotiations much easier. I was able to step back, be more disengaged emotionally, accept him and the situation, and see the not caring as a theme: he had brought me into his life, briefly, and when the project was over, I'd have my life back.

Hai, wakarimashita means that there is a potential delay, possibly a long one, in coming to a resolution. Rather than agreeing or disagreeing, the person saying *hai* is giving everyone a chance to think things through, to feel perhaps what the other person is feeling, to create a new relationship specific to the situation. During that time, in which a consensus is being built, you're not just thinking of your happiness. The thoughts and feelings of others matter as much or more than yours. This shift in thinking contributes to the ways in which Japanese society is organized.

On the other hand, with things going unsaid, with no decision reached—not yet, anyway—things can stagnate and get worse. In Japan there is a pattern of laissez-faire relatedness that has contributed to slow economic growth, indirectness that limits participation, social isolation, shame, exclusion of women from positions of civic and corporate authority, and very complicated marriage and dating patterns.

And yet the self-regard and self-improvement culture of the United States *also* creates a loss of identity and problems in each of the areas noted above. *What's in it for me and people who look like me?* When we are chiefly concerned about our own happiness, we loosen the threads that tie us to others in our families, communities, and places of work. That diminishment of empathy might create a momentary feeling of what passes for happiness, but it doesn't last. Wanting more for oneself can be a failure to accept the responsibility of living with others and taking care of those who need our help or cannot advocate for themselves.

When we lose that, it creates unhappiness, and while improving ourselves seems to be the solution to being unhappy, a lasting opportunity would be to make others happy and to experience satisfaction with them.

Maybe the best way to have well-being is to improve the lives of others.

Just sayin'.

Hai, wakarimashita is a way of listening, and understanding that creates possibilities for good decision making. You've acknowledged the other person. Saying *hai, wakarimashita* in our highly individualistic culture, in which too often there are winners and losers, can lead to acceptance of other people's points of views. It's the epitome of *ukeireru*.

Ukeireru is a way to minimize the anger, fear, and misery that arise from stressful situations. Understanding what's happening creates distance and a degree of calm disengagement. If you can say you understand, you're not reacting emotionally. You're thinking about what's happening and being said.

"Yes, I understand," takes things down a notch. Your needs and feelings and thoughts are no longer the most important things about the relationship. This is really liberating, and it gives you the authority to step back.

The need or desire to make communication, observation, and relatedness more meaningful applies not only to face-to-face situations. Many of us are interacting with friends and colleagues and strangers on the Internet. Without human contact, there's an odd freedom that has led to trolls, hate speech, and insults. Not quite as bad, but still pretty awful, is the aggressive tone that emails can take when making requests, providing feedback, and sharing observations.

Dr. Sherry Turkle, an MIT psychologist whose decades-long focus on the impact of technology on human behavior has yielded essential books on the psychological impact of technology, observed that empathy is decreased by our time in the virtual reality created by the Internet. That's certain to be true, and less time on the Internet would increase our actual awareness of the real needs of others. Dr. Turkle astutely notes the value of technology while at the same time analyzing keenly what happens to human beings when we spend more time on machines than ever before.

It is possible to limit time on the Internet while at home and in classrooms and restaurants, but it is probable that the future will include more communication, not less, in virtual reality. Like it or not, the Internet will increase its hold on the imagination and will attract more individuals and businesses that recognize its *monetary* and social advantages. It's not going away.

Horses were fun, but then there were cars.

I'm grateful to see people surfing the net on their phones while riding the subway. I can remember when equally bored individuals had no phones and annoyed people sitting next to them. People like me.

I can also remember the hassle of booking flights and hotel rooms via the mail or telephone. Or standing in crowded stores not sure if the price was fair for what I was buying and having no comparison at my fingertips. And taking hours to shop for stuff that I can now order in seconds from an array of websites to be delivered the next day to my home. With time freed up, I have more freedom to do other things like take a walk with Beau, run at the gym, read a book, write, cook a decent dinner, meet a friend for coffee, and so on.

We can all think of countless examples of how the Internet has enhanced our lives. Why not apply *Hai, wakarimashita* to the Internet and implement Dr. Turkle's profound concern for and understanding of empathy in virtual situations? Take the real and apply it to the virtual.

Emails and texts and social media postings in Japan, and back and forth with friends there, often have a tone that is pleasant and observational. As in: "I understand that it will be challenging to see you in New York, since my time there is short, but my disappointment may exceed yours. How might we meet another time?" Or: "I understand that you meant to get the files to me by Friday. Unfortunately, they are not here. What is the new timetable?" And: "Sorry to be a bother. It may be my misunderstanding, but did we agree that it was time to review the proposal? What are your thoughts?"

By admitting at the outset that you understand, you are implying that you didn't understand before.

Chapter Twelve

What Would Dogen Do?

The year is 1229, and Dogen doesn't know what to do. He's one of the monks in charge of a Zen Buddhist monastery in medieval Japan. It's freezing outside as well as indoors in the dead of winter, sweltering hot in summer, clammy and wet during rainy seasons. He has decided to write a guide on how to cook with instructions that will bring Zen teachings and principles into the kitchen. But how to go about it?

Healthy? Balanced? Nutritious? Delicious?

There are no doctors with valid, reliable knowledge that can help to diagnose let alone treat many preventable diseases. Palliation is limited. No medical institutions exist. No cooking schools, no nutritionists, few facts.

What there is of science consists largely of poesy and elegiac observations centered around nature, acceptance of the unknowable, and fostering the belief that pain and loss are what each of us can expect from life. Might as well.

Not much exists in the way of pain relief, deaths in childbirth are a common occurrence, and even if you make it past age five, good luck getting to thirty. No wonder Japanese culture embraced brevity and being at one with timeless mountains and forests, skies and oceans.

In order to face life's challenges with fortitude, Dogen figures, we need awareness. How to create that awareness is the responsibility of people like him: men who have removed themselves from everyday life and instead devote most of their waking hours to establishing calm that is necessary in order to be part of and accept nature.

What does nature want from us? How can we know? And once we kind of think we know, what can we do to meet expectations in order to be accepted by nature?

Little information is available for Dogen to pore through. No secular libraries, no public places where discussions are held, few open-ended conversations. How people relate to one another hasn't changed much, not over centuries, and it's through following a well-scripted set of memorized prayers and honorifics that people like him get through the day.

Outside the monastery, it's another story.

At least Dogen and his disciples have a sturdy, well-built place to live, fields to till, food to cook, and time to come up with ways to show acceptance.

Dogen made it to the ripe old age of fifty-three (1200–1253), but those outside the monastery were usually not so lucky. Life was hard and cruel. Exposed to nature's vicissitudes through inadequate housing, lacking basics like good shoes and durable clothing, unable to protect themselves against the natural disasters of floods and typhoons and hurricanes and volcanoes, prone to famines because of ignorance about agriculture, illiterate, and forced into war by feudal lords, the Japanese population of whom Dogen was supposed to be the spiritual leader needed all the help they could get.

There's not much Dogen could do—or wanted to do or occurred to him to do—about the systemic and institutional conditions that kept people down. Mired in centuries of repetition, habits informed by prayer, and flat-out efforts to survive, he wasn't the type.

Not only that: Zen was in bed with the feudal lords who gave them the funds they used to meditate on life without having to slog through fields, sleep in huts, or go off to fight in a war about which they knew nothing. In exchange, the Zen monks granted the feudal lords legitimacy. The lords were not only blessed by Zen Buddhism but viewed and accepted to be divine rulers. To defy them was an act against nature, inhuman, illogical, and unnatural.

Dogen chose to ally himself *with* nature as best he could, as best he knew how. Remarkably, what he thought and then wrote down, taking decades to do so, became the gold standard for Japanese cuisine. Remarkable because he proceeded without antecedents, regardless of legacy, independent of other thinkers, and in relative isolation. Where did his ideas and convictions come from?

From observation.

He had, if nothing else, time on his hands, and without a lot of books, none of them secular, and few obligations other than hours of murmured prayers and mindless chores, Dogen was free to take in the world, measure its expectations, and see where we might fit in. He could listen to his breathing, feel his body, and appreciate temporality.

What does the body want? How is our body accepting of nature?

Because he lived outside of the life led by most, from peasants who were often starving to lords who were often avaricious, Dogen could afford to be impractical. His outlook was anything but expedient. He wasn't clued in to what was possible and what was impossible. What he came up with instead was the embodiment of a dream, an ideal way of cooking.

What did Dogen do? "Dogen wrote that there are five flavors, five colors, and five ways to cook," Chef Masahiko Miura, of Mizuki restaurant in Kyoto, told me. "Five flavors: *kan* (sweet), *ku* (bitter), *kan* (salty), *san* (sour), and *shin* (spicy). Five colors: *aka* (red), *ao* (green), *ki* (yellow), *shiro* (white), and *kuro* (black). Finally, five ways to cook: *niru* (simmer), *mus* (steam), *ageru* (fry), *yaku* (grill), and *nama* (raw)."

If you're a peasant or a lord or even a Zen monk, these guidelines are *really* impractical. Poetic, to be sure, but useful?

"Look," Miura explained, "about eight hundred years ago, Dogen wrote an essay called the 'Tenzo Kyōkun.' He was a monk at a monastery; a *tenzo* is a cook. His essay is a guide to the proper way to cook, and up to today, the 'Tenzo Kyōkun' is the bible for all Japanese chefs. No document is comparable. The 'Tenzo Kyōkun' offers guidelines and has rules that still have meaning for professional cooks in modern Japan. Some of the guidelines are specific to *kaiseki* dining,* but even

---

* *Kaiseki* is a *kanji* word that means "stone in the bosom" and refers to a centuries-old practice that the Buddhist monks followed in the winter.

its basic philosophy is relevant to a culture in which guests sit at counters and watch chefs grill chicken or serve noodles: 'The *tenzo* must be present, paying careful attention to the rice and soup while they are cooking. This is true whether the *tenzo* does the work himself or has assistants helping him either with the cooking or the tending of the fires. Do not be negligent and careless just because the materials seem plain, and hesitate to work more diligently with materials of superior quality.'"

Dogen made it clear that it is necessary to be thoughtful about cooking, to consider what you are doing to ingredients, and whom you are feeding. You must accept that you are part of nature through the food.

Most Japanese don't make use of five flavors, five colors, and five ways of cooking when preparing a meal at home. It's a refined and time-consuming approach that you find in rarified atmospheres. To follow Dogen precisely, you had better be highly skilled, too.

The reason why Dogen is still meaningful today, even for those of us not working in elite kitchens or served by them, is that he introduced and formulated guidelines. These guidelines encourage us to think about how and what we eat, and

---

They placed hot stones under their robes to ward off the cold. Literally "heartwarming food." Not these days! Now it works like this: Multiple courses of very small amounts of intensely flavored food arrive in succession. The dishes are strictly seasonal and emphasize colors, presentation, texture, and heat. It's to Japanese food what haute cuisine is to French food: rare, rooted in aristocratic tradition, and currently a typical experience exclusively reserved for the rich.

they are applicable to any number of types of food, not just Japanese. Through Dogen, we are better able to observe, appreciate, and accept nature.

The diet in Dogen's era was chiefly vegetarian. For monks and lords, this could mean high-end *shojin ryori* (the traditional vegetarian approach of Zen Buddhist cooking) on occasion. For most everyone else, it was greens and gruel. (Fish and marine species were often exempted, if you had access.) It wasn't until 1872 that the Meiji emperor said it was OK to eat beef, and while in previous centuries pig farming and hunting existed, the daily diet for peasants was simple. It was, in large measure, a diet of subsistence.

When you're eating to survive, like a peasant, or even eating to show off, like a lord, the food isn't bound up with nature. *You* bring meaning to the food in both instances. You don't allow the food to be experienced as *it* was meant in nature. You impose your needs and desires.

People around the globe associate Japanese food with amazing and expensive items, like sushi, or with luxury meals, like *kaiseki*, and with delicious bowls of *ramen* or *udon* or *soba*. Food tours in Japan take foreign guests to three-star Michelin restaurants, terrific *yakitori* joints, *izakaya*, *yakiniku*, *tempura*, *soba*, *udon*, *tonkatsu*, and upscale steak restaurants where dinner for two can easily run to a thousand dollars. But Japanese cuisine, before and during the time of Dogen, and up through about 1972, was made up of foods that reflected a nation in various stages of poverty and isolation.

In *Japan's Dietary Transition and Its Impacts*, co-author Dr. Kazuhiko Kobayashi, a former professor of agriculture at Tokyo University, described how throughout Japan's history the food stayed simple because the nation lagged behind in agricultural production.

As late as 1920, people throughout Japan barely had enough to eat. Dr. Kobayashi quotes "the recollections of Ihara Orinosuke," born in 1904. These recollections are described in *Memories of Silk and Straw: A Self-Portrait of Small-Town Japan*, a book written by Junichi Saga: "In our village a meal of a mixture of rice and barley, with six parts barley to four parts rice, would've been considered above average. . . . Fresh river fish we almost never had up in the mountain where I lived. . . . We never saw any fresh sea fish, either, from one year to the next. But at New Year most families bought one salted salmon, though only after an awful fuss."

Talk about *Jiro Dreams of Sushi*!

What, sushi? There's gruel. You want gruel? We got gruel. No sushi, no poultry, no pork, no beef.[*]

For all the excitement these days about rice as a symbol of Japan and a constant in much of the cuisine, Dr. Kobayashi

---

[*]Dr. Kobayashi notes that in 1900 in Japan, "Egg production averaged only one egg per person every month. . . . The Buddhist proscription of animal killing led to increasingly stringent bans on eating animal foods, although fish and other marine species were always exempt . . . and a variety of meat substitutes using tofu and wheat gluten."

quotes research showing that "rice became the staple only in 1939 with the advent of food rationing."

Rice, Dr. Kobayashi writes, was more *symbolic* of "wealth, power, and beauty" than part of most people's diet. And perhaps because it was a fantasy, its unrealistic place in Japanese imagination elevated its meaning.

This was Dogen's world: gruel for most people who were lucky to live past the age of thirty and luxe, lavish food on occasions for the fortunate few who maintained the conditions and institutions responsible for widespread poverty.

Dr. Kobayashi and I had a couple of dinners together on cold, black evenings in Tokyo. We sat on mats in a local pub near his university offices and talked over *sake* and fresh fish, steamed vegetables, and bowls of noodles in hot broth.

Dr. Kobayashi is a shy, thoughtful person, with a shock of white hair, a swift stride from years of bicycling to work, a rumpled suit, and a sly grin. He is an extraordinary listener who absorbs words and waits awhile before stating his views, which are usually more factual than opinionated. These days he is researching organic rice production in Japan, China, and Vietnam.

I had cause, as usual, for celebrating the simplicity of Japanese food and told him how I appreciated the coaxing of flavors, the connection of the food to nature, and the general absence of sauces. I told him that I especially loved the very natural tastes: unadorned raw fish, mountain herbs, seasonal products, soft tofu with shredded ginger and a drop of soy, and so on.

He pushed back his eyeglasses. We sat in silence for a few moments.

"Japan was poor," Dr. Kobayashi said. "The food is simple because we had no money for centuries. Japan was broke!"

Picture Dogen. Inventive yet loyal to tradition and set in his ways through texts and prayers, he arrives at patterns of colors, tastes, and ways of cooking that eight hundred years later are ways of seeing and being that many of us still think about.

Although I've worked for several years in three restaurants in Boston and New York City, I'm not a professional cook. At home I cook simple food with good ingredients, choosing from about two dozen or so recipes I've memorized and tried to improve on.

Night after night, I cook Japanese, Italian, and North American food, from decent *dashi* to *cacio e pepe* to grilled tuna to cheeseburgers.

Where Dogen comes in is the thought taking place as I cook, how slowly or quickly I cook, what the food will look like on the plate, and how the food is prepared: *niru* (simmer), *musu* (steam), *ageru* (fry), *yaku* (grill), and *nama* (raw). Taking the time to decide what to cook, how to cook it, thinking about the preferences of those I'm serving, and how to serve it means that I am deliberating—I'm relating both to the food and the people I'm cooking for long before anyone's had a bite.

This also means thinking about how animals are raised and slaughtered and considering the impact on nature of consumption. I rarely eat out in the town* where I live. Then, too, cooking at home means I can control the amount of salt and sugar.†

Thinking a lot about food means trying to understand that it's not just about me. Animal welfare, environmental impact, physical health, wages for employees, the cultural and economic implications of private equity taking over both high- and low-end restaurants, and mental health of restaurant workers all enter as contexts. You ignore these contexts at your own peril.

Don't get me wrong: I want to be well-fed, and I love a good Jamaican patty or a Philadelphia cheesesteak. I don't turn to local produce or organic food shipped from Costa Rica, necessarily, though I'm cooking far more vegetarian dishes than ever. The fact is that we all spend more time buying and preparing food than actually eating it. So why not add more contexts to our appreciation of what's on the plate?

This outlook is not original, and when you read folks like Michael Pollan, for sure he is way, way, way ahead of me in

---

*As far as I'm concerned, pizza is not eating out. In Boston, Galleria Umberto, my favorite restaurant in the city, bar none, serves arguably the country's best square Sicilian slice, no toppings on offer. I feel confident knowing that if Dogen were alive today, in Boston on a book tour, that he would greet Ralph and Paul Deuterio, the pizzeria's owners, as Zen masters.

†A well-known chef in Boston added to my understanding of this when she said, "The difference between a four-star restaurant and others is a box of salt."

his understanding and expertise. We get to the same place in different ways.

And if you are inclined to make even more practical changes to your home cooking that connect you to Japanese traditions, as well as the thoughts and feelings attendant to that, why not pick up some cookbooks that can teach you how to do it?

I have four favorite Japanese cookbooks.

Japanese Cooking: A Simple Art, by Shizuo Tsuji, has an introduction by M. F. K. Fisher, the great food writer. This classic highlights the spiritual essence of the food. Fisher writes: "One immediate result of this intense experience [of eating *ryori* in Japan] is that when I cook for myself now, I am increasingly simple in both the sources of food and its preparation, and when I must eat in other houses or restaurants, I find the dishes heavy and over flavored, and the supplies not fresh enough." In addition to the philosophical underpinnings, Tsuji's book is easy to use, and I rely upon it weekly.

Another great work is *The Japanese Kitchen*, by Hiroko Shimbo, which offers step-by-step, easy-to-follow recipes for cooking at home.

Washoku, by Elizabeth Andoh, is an encyclopedic book that is as educational as it is useful. No book captures better the meanings of traditional Japanese food.

The most recent entry is very beautiful to look at and hold: *Japanese Farm Food*, by Nancy Singleton Hachisu. If you want to understand how to prepare comfort food the Japanese way, with an emphasis on vegetables, this is your book. Recipes include grilled tofu pouches with ginger and scallions, young scallions with miso, and mountain vegetable tempura.

Dogen did not invent thoughtful cooking, but since he came up with his guidelines long ago, during times of crushing poverty, his work is informed by a need to connect to nature, to make use of the little he had, and *to accept our place in the world through a relationship to those ingredients that sustain our lives.*

It's an approach to cuisine that is all the more remarkable because it originated and evolved from a monastery rather than a cooking school, restaurant, or royal court.

Dogen was inspired by awareness of life's brevity and was concerned that we are cut off from nature by our grievances, worries, anger, and disappointments. Not enough to eat? Life is too short for rich and poor? Eat in accordance with nature. *Accept* what you have by making the most of it.

In Japan today, with its vast modernity and extraordinary but very recent wealth as a nation, *absolute* evidence of Dogen's edicts is rare. You can experience *shojin ryori* cuisine, the traditional vegetarian approach of Zen Buddhist cooking, at restaurants and *ryokan* where meals are served and eaten slowly and prepared painstakingly. With precision and slowing down, this is food that demands your attention. Observing the serving vessels, how each one is laid out on a table, the hands of a server positioning the dishes, by the time you actually lift morsels of food into your mouth you've already been removed from reality and its stimuli unrelated to the act of eating.

Then, too, there's ultra-refined, rare, and very expensive *kaiseki* meals. You're nobody compared to that firefly shrimp glistening and translucent, not as vital as mountain herbs found by the chef that morning under a fresh layer of late spring snow.

To call oneself a *kaiseki* or *shojin ryori* chef in Japan takes years and years of apprenticeship, acceptance by mentors, and recognition by peers. Few have the skill or nerve to do it. Often, a *kaiseki* chef is the latest scion in a family business, going back for generations.

Because these kinds of eating are usually so elaborate or expensive, many Japanese do not experience them. But the food that people in Japan *do* eat on a regular, daily basis has a relationship to what Dogen laid down as law. Acknowledging the foreign origins of *ramen* and *gyoza* (Chinese), *tempura* (Portuguese), curry (Indian), and *yakiniku* (Korean), and understanding the tastes of *yakitori, soba, sushi,* and steamed vegetables, the adherence to color, the variation of taste, and the focus on texture via cooking method, contribute to an increased awareness of what's on the plate. That awareness can inspire thinking about where the food came from and how we are connected to these sources.

Awareness of food as part of everyday life, not just sustenance, starts early in Japan, and of course if thinking a lot more about what we eat and why we eat was part of our lives here to a greater degree, and institutionalized and made systemic, our kids might be healthier.

In Japan, a healthy approach to eating starts in childhood at school. School lunches (known as *kyushoku*) are developed in each prefecture by nutritionists and dieticians. These are put into place in public elementary schools. Most junior high schools also serve school lunches, but in those districts where lunch is not provided, parents have to prepare food at home for them. Students in senior high schools either bring food from home or buy some on the way in convenience stores or from vendors' stalls on school grounds.

School lunches are rooted in Japanese cultural traditions: "The first school lunch in Japan was started by a Buddhist monk who oversaw a school in Tsuruoka City, Yamagata Prefecture. The idea to provide lunch at school came about when he noticed that many of the disadvantaged children weren't coming to school with packed lunches from home. These first simple lunches consisted of *onigiri* (rice balls), grilled fish, and *tsukemono* (pickled vegetables). Word spread about the success of the monk's school lunch program. Before long, schools around the country had embraced the idea and were beginning to offer lunches to their students as well. Rice mixed with meat and/or vegetables, fish, and varieties of miso soup became typical food items found on the menus."

School lunches in Japan became so much a part of what it means to educate a child that in 1954 the government enacted a School Lunch Act: "School lunch was recognized as a legitimate part of children's education as a way to teach knowledge about how food is produced and important dining customs," according to a 2015 article in *Japan Times*.

When I asked my friend Yumi, whose husband is a pediatrician, about school lunches of her childhood and of her two sons, she told me, "You may want to know that aside from the lunch served, eating, chewing, and drinking are strictly prohibited at school at least until grade nine. If they are thirsty, they should drink tap water. Not even a candy, not even a piece of chocolate, no soft drinks are tolerated."

OK, but what exactly *are* the kids eating?

Menus vary from prefecture to prefecture, based on seasons and local products: balance, freshness, and small portions. *Nourishing Japan*, a website that focuses on Japanese school lunches, lists a range of typical school lunches, which invariably include a protein (fish, soybeans, chicken, liver), a starch (noodles or rice), and two vegetables. A Japanese school lunch is organized, in part, by color. *Nourishing Japan* notes:

> The Japanese have concocted their own way to teach children about their food. . . . They've grouped it into three categories: red, yellow and green. This group of three is regularly included in the school lunch menu explanation:
>
> **RED:** Chicken, tofu, milk, herring and seaweed
>
> **YELLOW:** Rice, potato, flour, yam, and mayonnaise
>
> **GREEN:** Carrots, burdock root, soybeans, Napa cabbage, cucumber, daikon, and dried mushrooms.

I thought of Dogen and his colors.

"Is this true, Yumi? Is this typical?"

"Yes," Yumi explained. "Red for protein, yellow for carbohydrates, and green for vitamin. We remember these foods by their functions, namely, food that builds our body (protein), food that generates energy (carbohydrates), and food that conditions our body (vitamins). I remember that when I was in school, at lunchtime, announcements were made over the loud speaker about the day's menu and what nutrition can be obtained from which food."

There is something, too, that informs and organizes Japanese school lunches: outside of allergies or medical concerns, Yumi told me that individual food preferences are considered a selfish act, that the person is felt to be trying to separate rather than accept his or her place in the group.

"You may also want to know that at the beginning of each month," she said patiently, "the printed menu for the coming weeks is given to the parents so that they will know what their kids will be eating at school each day and what they should cook for dinner to supplement the nutrients."

Families, through this practice, become an extension of the school. There is less separation: children are inescapably a part of a total system meant to show that, as a group in school and at home, parents and teachers are working together. (Like it or not, kids!)

"To behave properly, it is not enough not to insist on foods one is fond of; it is required that one eat foods that are disliked," Gail Benjamin, noted American anthropologist writes. "Health may be improved by this, but moral character definitely is—selfishness rooted out, sincerity and cooperation exhibited and attained."

Japanese continue thinking about food from childhood into the adult years through careful categorization of what's on the plate, giving new meaning to the phrase "You are what you eat." Like other countries and religions, the culture recognizes how food conveys belonging, a kind of tribalism, and a way to show affiliation.

Two terms for food eaten in Japan are *yoshoku* and *washoku*. Food writer and longtime friend and Tokyoite Robb Satterwhite, whose website, bento.com, is one of the best sources about dining in Japan, told me, "The word *yoshoku* is extremely ambiguous and heavily context-dependent. Personally, I would only use it to refer to the very specific Japanese *yoshoku* restaurant cuisine that includes curry rice, fried-rice omelets, Hamburg steak, and deep-fried prawns."

Washoku is a term used to define "purely" Japanese food. So important is *washoku* to the overall cuisine that UNESCO in 2013 placed it on the Representative List of the Intangible Cultural Heritage of Humanity. UNESCO defines *washoku* as "a social practice based on a set of skills, knowledge, practice and traditions related to the production, processing, preparation and consumption of food. It is associated with an essential spirit of respect for nature that is closely related to the sustainable use of natural resources."

Kind of vague, right? And I wonder what Dogen would do. But what he probably would appreciate, if I have the temerity to guess what a Zen Buddhist monk who lived eight hundred years ago would think, is that there is something important about cuisine that has "respect for nature that is closely related to the sustainable use of natural resources."

Take *washoku* as a principle from Dogen, and apply it to your own home cooking; show respect for nature in what you eat. Yes, colors, tastes, and cooking methods are essential, and their meaning is deepened when understood within the context of respect and sustainability.

Cooking and eating food that adds to your awareness of nature and helps you to accept where you fit in has a restorative, calming effect. You can begin to realize that it's not about you, it's not even about the food—it's about creating understanding of the need to accept life's brevity and how food hastens our demise while at the same time sustaining us.

A thoughtful approach also applies to sugar, salt, calories, and lifestyle.

According to Professors Vaclav Smil and Kazuhiko Kobayashi, writing in *Japan's Dietary Transition and Its Impacts*, "Japan's sugar supply has remained very low when compared to both other affluent nations and some low-income countries. . . . It still derives less food energy from sugar than any other affluent country."

Although we cannot give full credit to Dogen for the positive features of eating in modern Japan, from healthy and balanced school lunches to an emphasis in many homes on seasonal cooking, he got the ball rolling by writing a book that demands that people think about what they are eating and consider its spiritual implications. And perhaps most importantly, let's remember Dogen's purpose.

He was living during a time when everything was pretty much decided at birth. Expectations of ordinary people, to the extent that one dared to hope, centered on survival.

Dogen created rules that exist today and have important and specific features we can bring to our lives.

By establishing categories of color-taste-cooking methodology, he broke through the isolation of being an individual. He created shared experiences, which add a lot to what it means to be accepted in a community and as part of nature.

He directed his attention and efforts to others and to observation. His book isn't a compendium of elitism, like Escoffier, and it isn't specific in terms of what to eat. The idea was—and is—to think about how you are cooking, in terms of methods, colors, and tastes, and know that any number of dishes can emerge, no matter who you are or where you live. Just think, anticipate, and respect the possibility that eating, *through its baseness*, brings us closer to nature and to one another.

I mean, after all, isn't that what Dogen would do?

Chapter
Thirteen

How to Make a Decision

Like many people, I often find it extremely hard to make decisions.

Sitting in front of a blank screen and trying to decide what to write a page or two about is a task that may take weeks. I comfort myself by saying that at least I showed up, that I'm thinking about the work, and that the pain and terror and shame of being indecisive are part of the decision-making process.

That kind of works for a while. Or doesn't.

Even when it doesn't work, I can still say to myself that no one is forcing me to do this, and that this is the life I've chosen.

I also rely on a bunch of quotes or sayings that help me to see that I'm not alone. These help me to feel as if I am part of a group, accepted by them, and to realize that others face similar and far more painful, difficult challenges. My struggles are not unique; I'm not important. Then, too, the quotes focus on the work rather than on the person doing the work. They help me to accept the situation.

Japanese students and families display in homes and in schools an array of quotes, prayers, sayings, and edicts meant to inspire and create a sense of group cohesion.

Yuki Kojima, a friend from Japan now living in Boston, taught me more about these sayings than what I had known before. Between running tours to *sake kura* (breweries) in various prefectures, Yuki is bringing Japanese culture to this city.

"Some people in Japan have a hanging scroll to display calligraphy words," she told me. "They may not be there to cheer yourself, but rather it is to make you think. I've seen calligraphy of *'ichigo-ichiei'* or *'shikisoku zeku'* on the wall of Japanese houses, for example."

Imagine an American home with something comparable—"Now or Never" or "Here Today, Gone Tomorrow"—and you get a stark sense of the big difference between the cultures.

Ichigo-ichiei means that what's happening now is not going to happen again, not in the same way, so it's a really good idea to immerse yourself in the experience and pay close attention.

As for *shikisoku zeku*, according to the website Form Is Itself Voidness, the term "indicates the idea that all things, including matter, the human mind, and events, originate from the same foundation. Though these things seem to be different from one another in the eyes of man, their real state is equal. When analyzed to the utmost possible limit, all things are equal because they are energy (force) of some kind. . . .

In short, all phenomena are produced from an equal kind of energy or force."

Adopting the point of view that "all things, including matter, the human mind, and events, originate from the same foundation" means that *we* impose the differences that separate us from one another and nature. The reality, however, is that our origins (and demise) are the same. Equality ought to be a salve, a way to accept the fact that *we are separated from nature for less time than we are part of it*, and therefore we are literally joined to one another.

Yuki also told me about banners that students in Japan hang in their college dorm rooms:

Ganbare 頑張れ! (Good luck)

Hisho 必勝! (Certain Victory)

Like the sayings in homes, the slogans students rely on are not about selfish concerns. *Good luck* and *certain victory* apply to whoever reads them. It's not: "Be all *you* can be," or, "Be the best version of *you*," or "If *you* can dream it, *you* can achieve it," or, "Yes, *you* can."

Yuki also told me about a poem written by Kenji Miyazawa in 1931 that, she said, "everyone in Japan has to learn in middle school."

雨ニモマケズ
風ニモマケズ
雪ニモ夏ノ暑サニモマケヌ
丈夫ナカラダヲモチ
慾ハナク
決シテ瞋ラズ
イツモシヅカニワラッテヰル
一日ニ玄米四合ト
味噌ト少シノ野菜ヲタベ
アラユルコトヲ
ジブンヲカンジョウニ入レズニ
ヨクミキキシワカリ
ソシテワスレズ
野原ノ松ノ林ノ蔭ノ
小サナ萱ブキノ小屋ニヰテ
東ニ病氣ノコドモアレバ
行ッテ看病シテヤリ
西ニツカレタ母アレバ
行ッテソノ稲ノ束ヲ負ヒ
南ニ死ニサウナ人アレバ
行ッテコハガラナクテモイヽトイヒ
北ニケンクヮヤソショウガアレバ
ツマラナイカラヤメロトイヒ
ヒデリノトキハナミダヲナガシ
サムサノナツハオロオロアルキ
ミンナニデクノボートヨバレ
ホメラレモセズ
クニモサレズ
サウイフモノニ
ワタシハナリタイ

Not defeated by the rain
Not defeated by the wind
With a strong body to fight against the snow
And the heat of summer
Not greedy
Not angry at anyone
Always gently smiling
Eat four cups of brown rice and miso daily
With some vegetables
Put others before yourself
Listen well and understand
Not forgetful
Live in a small thatched hut
Under the shade of pine trees in the field
When there is a sick child to the east
Go and take care of him
When there is an exhausted mother to the west
Go and carry her bundles of rice plants
When there is a dying person to the south
Go and say there is no need to be afraid
When there is an argument or a lawsuit to the north
Go and tell them not to waste their time
In times of drought
Shed tears
In a cold summer
Wander aimlessly
Be called useless
Receive no praises
Receive no complaints
Such a person
I want to become

(TRANSLATED BY YUKI KOJIMA)

Lines like, "Put others before yourself / Listen well and understand" offer a way out of loneliness. By putting others ahead of your needs, by listening, and by trying to understand, you base your concerns on relationships rather than personal satisfaction. Happiness isn't mentioned.

Lines like "When there is an exhausted mother to the west / Go and carry her bundles of rice plants / . . . When there is a fight or a lawsuit to the north / Go and tell them not to waste their time" demonstrate specifically what can and ought to be done in order to become a better person. The recommended actions also show that a community exists along with common cause and a web of relationships.

Then, too, "Go and tell them not to waste their time" suggests that by helping others, the speaker is providing an example of how to tamp down conflicts and that others will perhaps listen to his or her advice.

By accepting the importance of empathy, recognizing the value of community, and putting others' needs before one's own, one becomes a better, more decisive person. The decisions are based on how they are of benefit to others, not by looking for personal happiness from making a decision, which is regarded as selfish.

That Japanese kids between the ages of twelve and fourteen are forced to memorize this poem means that they have in their heads some words that can help to guide them during adolescence. These aren't magic words, they don't always work, but they do serve as a reminder that the natural selfishness of being a human being isn't the goal.

This is the goal: "Receive no praises, / Receive no complaints, / Such a person / I want to become." Struggles like "Who am I?," which is the hallmark question of being a teenager, are in part resolved: I'm someone who takes care of others, is part of a community, feels protected knowing that others in the community will take care of me if I need their help, and is capable of making things better.

Accepting the group's values as more important than one's own contributes to the well-being of Japanese through systems and institutions that focus on public infrastructure, public health care, equality in wealth distribution, and access to medical care. The development and maintenance of these come about in part as a result of an outlook emphasizing groups. That outlook starts at an early age and continues throughout childhood and adolescent development. It's based on acceptance of vulnerability and a strong need for individuals to do something about that.

How does your decision affect others?

I have eight quotations or sayings pinned to my bulletin board, which is about five feet from my desk, that I've had there for decades and that I look at all the time.

Here is one quotation by Anna Akhmatova that helps me make decisions:

One day somebody in the crowd identified me. Standing behind me was a woman, with lips blue from cold, who had, of course, never heard me called by name before. Now she started out of the torpor common to us all and asked me in a whisper (everyone whispered there): "Can you describe this?"

And I said: "I can."

Then something like a smile passed fleetingly over what had once been her face.

Akhmatova was a famous Russian poet, and what she is describing is the time when her son Lev was incarcerated in Kresty prison (in what was then Leningrad) by order of Stalin for nearly a year and a half. She stood waiting for news each day during his imprisonment, along with all the hundreds of others whose fathers, husbands, and sons had been put in prison for political reasons.

Was Lev dead? Was Lev living? Not a word. Can you imagine if Lev was your child?

Because she was famous, people recognized and approached her with a hope that her literary authority might be a balm.

If Akhmatova had decided to describe how *she* felt, the pain *she* was in, the impossibility of that introspection might have overwhelmed her.

How can anyone think *primarily* about individual suffering when others are suffering, too?

Akhmatova's description of her tragic predicament and her extraordinary courage help me to understand that my decisions, meaningless in comparison, are part of a more important struggle to be a decent human being.

People I evaluate often don't have the words to describe their lives—they are in too much pain—but maybe I can do it on their behalf. I have countless examples of the privilege of being trusted enough to hear intimacies, aware of falling short, not understanding enough, or not at all, but at least not being afraid, like most others in that person's life, of hearing the ongoing terror, and trying for the two of us to put it into words or accept it through a shared silence in a room together, however briefly.

Then, too, when I write, I'm trying to create and document things that might matter to readers who share my doubts and misgivings but don't have the words *yet*.

I feel as if I have a purpose or mission that has nothing to do with me. I'm just the messenger. This type of inclusive, empathic thinking helps with all kinds of decision making. I try to steer clear of the them-against-us, true-false, best-way-to-do-things, argumentative, my-way-or-the-highway kind of thinking.

When you realize that acceptance of the group's needs comes first, it opens up innovative ways to make decisions with others. If you take yourself out of the situation, you're halfway there. No matter what the situation, from serious to mundane, I find that asking this question is a good place to start: "How are *we* going to solve this challenge?"

It's no longer a problem being described; it's a challenge. And, more importantly, both of you are facing it together. You're on the same side. The idea that the two of you are working on the same challenge shows that you're open to resolving things, see the other person's points of view, and perhaps have some of the same goals.

When this *doesn't* work, and things remain stuck, another way to demonstrate that you and your would-be adversary are part of the same group, rather than individuals, is to say this: "If you were me, what would you do?"

If a conversation follows the question, with details, slowly, and with lots of observation and empathy, the person with whom you are having a conflict *might* see your point of view. They may not suggest a solution that you're comfortable with, but at the very least they now perhaps understand and even accept the validity of your position. And when they put themselves in your place, and state what they would do, you are better able to see *their* point of view.

A third question that helps with decision making adds a key feature: "How have you solved challenges like this before?" What worked, and what didn't? Chances are the problem you're having isn't likely to be original, and when it's happened before to other people, different, successful approaches were taken.

The best decisions are often made with three strategies I experienced in Japan:

Consider the impact on others of the decision.
Consider if the best decision is not to decide at that moment.
Have deep awareness of the sources of the thoughts and
    emotions informing the decision.

Strategies for both private and public decision making, inspired by cohesiveness, acceptance of others, and selflessness, decrease stress and loneliness. David Creswell and Emily Lindsay, two psychologists who studied the impact of loneliness and the pain it causes, concluded that "subjects whose training included acceptance and equanimity were measurably more sociable."

Acceptance of others, awareness of the pain they are in, is central to decision making.

Chapter
Fourteen

Read the Air

Shinji has settled into an armchair in the shadowy lounge on a high floor of a fancy hotel overlooking the moats and vast gardens of the Imperial Palace in Tokyo. The sun is setting, it's late November, and I'm seated beside my old friend.

We've been served a couple of tall beers by a waiter who didn't seem to lift his feet when he glided to us from the bar. An Oscar Peterson CD is playing softly from that direction, barely audible, but if we listen closely, the Gershwin tune is recognizable: "I Was Doing All Right."

After touching the rims of our glasses together—"Cheers!"—the two of us lean back at the same time and look at the glass wall, ceiling to floor, that offers a panoramic view. The place is empty, and although we only see one another at most a few times each year, neither of us says a word.

Shinji is a famous food guide. We spent the day eating but not talking much except about the food: who prepared it, where it came from, how to eat it, and so on. I nearly got in trouble with him the night before at a new restaurant that's all the rage called *Den*. I couldn't finish my rice.

"Please eat all your rice! It's an insult to the chef to leave even one grain," he had whispered. "I can see that you're stuffed, but please do it for me. I'm a regular here, and I want to be able to come back. Frankly, I wouldn't tell another Westerner this, but I know you will understand why it's important. Just do it!"

There's a lot I want to say to him *now*, and ask him about, but the silence doesn't allow it.

I look over at Shinji: He's got his usual beatific smile. With his dyed orange hair and big, round face, he reminds me of the Cheshire cat.

It used to be, when I first started coming to Japan about twenty years ago, that the silence of which I am now a part with Shinji would be disconcerting. Then I would fidget. Wonder what to say. Think I'm doing something wrong, missing cultural cues, not fitting in with Japanese etiquette.

Now I know better.

The silence *is* the etiquette. We're absorbing our surroundings, taking things in, appreciating the faint sounds of a piano playing, watching the sky darken. And just as importantly, our old friendship allows for this and creates the right tempo and atmosphere that make it possible to join the world around us.

So I'm not surprised when twenty minutes later, Shinji says, "So nice to be here at this moment."

That's it, except for a bow of my head.

I think back to times in Japan strongest in my memory. Again and again, I would sit with friends in silence, and it was often more satisfying that those times when conversation took place. Each time felt like the first time I had met the person because of our attentiveness toward one another, but at the same time the observations were deepened by years and years of familiarity.

Jiro and I are drinking coffee in the salon of his *ryokan* in the dead of winter. I've finished breakfast, I've gone to the hot springs, and I'm prepared to spend the day with him, interviewing farmers and artisans who provide things to the *ryokan*, from rice to soy sauce to eggs to lacquerware to paper made from tree bark to wooden bowls and chopsticks. The interviews will be in a booklet that Jiro will use to promote the property and offer to guests. I am waiting to hear our schedule, what he has mapped out—after all, we only have five days to do this and twenty people to meet.

But not a word.

We have each been given tiny French presses filled with hot water and freshly ground coffee that comes from Cuba. I know it's from Cuba because before Jiro showed up in the salon, Hiroshi, the barista, described in such extraordinary detail every fact he knew about the beans that I almost felt as if the coffee had some deeper, hidden meaning for him.

Hiroshi senses my thoughts without me saying anything, laughs shyly, and says, "I know, I know, I can get a little *otaku*."

Otaku is a term in Japan used to refer to individuals who go overboard with their interests to the point sometimes where their unrealistic outlook can lead to an unrealistic way of life. Like the guy who runs *Zoetrope*, a tiny bar in Tokyo with hundreds of bottles of rare Japanese whiskies. Or the odd young men who crowd around people dressed up in the *Akihabara* district as their favorite *anime* characters.

"No, Hiroshi," I say, "you're not *otaku*. You just love talking about coffee."

He bows a little and says, perhaps ironically, "Thank you for understanding."

Jiro removes his beautiful gold-frame eyeglasses, folds them so that the metal makes a faint, almost musical sound, and closes his eyes. When he opens his eyes, he says very softly, almost in a whisper, "Before we get started, I just want to tell you how much I appreciate this opportunity for us to work together."

I know the honorifics, the script, so I say, waiting about fifteen seconds and breathing deeply, "I want to thank you for trusting me to do this work with you. I'll do my best."

"Thank you," he says, and bows his head forward.

Then more silence, until Jiro opens a worn leather briefcase with his initials stenciled in gold just above the one central clasp. He takes out a sheer plastic folder and places copies of the day's schedule in front of both of us on the low table. He points to each appointment, indicated by name and location and precisely allotted time.

He says, "Shall we?"

Off we go.

The discussion—what to ask the artisans, what he hopes for in terms of the work, how this booklet will be organized— goes on unspoken. Even the few emails we exchanged before this morning were vague. But, believe me, I understand: I can tell from his gestures, and above all *his trust*, that we share the same goals.

We are experiencing a bit of *kuuki wo yomu*, which means "to read the air" or to sense and accept the other person's thoughts and feelings.

The silence in Japan isn't limited to friends. Civil suits are not common, and judges in civil courts are known to criticize both the accused and the accuser for not settling matters independently of the judicial system. Both parties are felt to be at fault for being unable to accept and resolve matters between themselves. This would be a good thing to adopt more of in the United States, which is in the top five of litigious countries in the world, preceded by, in order, Germany, Sweden, Israel, and Austria.*

Western nations are out of sync when it comes to con- flict resolution, and Japan's conflict-avoidant approach of- fers a way out: if you can observe other people's points of views, see things the way they see them, think a little bit more of what they might be thinking in addition to what *you* think, and feel what's in their hearts, at the very least all

---

*Though it must be said that more civil suits in Japan are advisable since there's been limited action against companies like Tepco and Chisso, which wreaked environmental havoc and caused human deaths.

that may serve to tamp down *your* anger and *your* needs and *your* frustration. And once your defenses are down, chances are you can come closer to a resolution that is acceptable to all concerned. Japanese make use of this strategy of conflict avoidance in daily life. Businesses are opening that tap into this cultural tradition.*

Avoiding conflict isn't the right choice in every situation, but it's nice to know that it's an option: In Case of Emergency, Don't Break Glass.

One of the best books that goes a long way toward explaining the "values and virtues" of Japanese understanding and how it helps resolve conflicts in relationships is *Japaneseness*, written by Yoji Yamakuse, which is the pen name of Hiroshi Kagawa. He writes, "Japanese can get their point across with a limited number of words. Avoiding conflict, being mindful

---

*Exit, a new Tokyo-based company run by Yuichiro Okazaki and Toshi-yuki Niino, offers employees a chance to quit without having to tell the boss themselves. "For a fee of 50,000 yen ($457), Exit will call a client's boss and deliver a resignation by proxy. Okazaki estimates that there are probably 30 companies offering a similar service in Japan." Imagine a similar service in the United States: no drama, no confrontation, just, "Hi, this is Bob from Exit. Just calling on behalf of Mary Wilson. She quits!" This takes away some of the authority of the employer while preserving the emotional well-being of the employee. A lot of people stay at horrible jobs just to avoid the stress of saying, "I quit." But in Japan, as in the United States, "in recent years more people have been switching jobs and the shrinking labor force means it's also a job-seekers' market." Enter Exit: "People are changing but the culture is not changing and also companies are not changing . . . and so that's why people need us," says Okazaki.

of others, creating a basis for mutual cooperation—these are the foundation of the Japanese approach."

One result of this different way of experiencing life is that it opens up the *probability* of building a group that protects and accepts everyone in it. The time it takes to figure out what is best for the group can decrease tensions.

Yamakuse describes *sukoshi ma o oite*, which he defines as "take a little break" and is said between people before things get heated. "Even within a single conversation," Yamakuse writes, "Japanese like to take breaks, allowing for periods of silence." During these "periods of silence" a lot is often going on even though you can't see or hear it. Yamakuse writes about inner strength: *ki*, which he describes as "an energy that cannot be seen," and *ki*'s relationship to *sakki*, defined as "sensing danger." What happens during wordless times is that this energy is conveyed between people. "It's so that he or she can now send his or her message to you without using words," he writes. "This sounds like the stuff of comics or movies, but . . . Japanese expect to be able to express their feelings to others without using words."

When I met with Yamakuse at his offices in Tokyo, he came across as both shy and assertive—a world-class listener who, while we sipped hot green tea from little ceramic cups brought to us on a small tray by one of his assistants, seemed to be able to read me without my having to say much.

It was cold out, early December. We spoke about the complexities of interaction that take place between people, East and West. Yamakuse consults for Japanese as well as Western businesses on how to make headway in dealings.

How to fit in culturally. How to express oneself in Western settings for Japanese and how Westerners can make themselves understood in Japan.

But it was the silences between us that created opportunities to exchange a few words with one another about family matters even though we had just met. I think we just accepted one another a little.

Chapter
Fifteen

Contentment

We live in a country in which personal happiness is said to be an entitlement. Why, it's right there in the Declaration of Independence!

> We hold these truths to be self-evident, that all men are created equal, that they are endowed by their Creator with certain unalienable Rights, that among these are Life, Liberty and the pursuit of Happiness.

No wonder so many people want to come here. How many other countries are founded on the basis of having an inalienable right to pursue happiness?

The men who wrote that in 1776 were indeed thinking about their inalienable right to pursue happiness, and they no doubt convinced themselves that they were well on their way. Never mind the unhappiness of the enslaved and the disenfranchised. Those were not their concerns.

But is it too much to suggest that these framers of a new nation might have been more *content* in a society in which these inalienable rights of theirs weren't exclusive? Imagine then the country that would have been established.

With the help of psychotherapists, psychopharmacology, life coaches, personal trainers, self-help books, mindfulness workshops, and an array of techniques, people in the West are well on their way, once again, to pursuing happiness. Many of these approaches are of enormous value—why *not* be happy?

But why not go *beyond* happiness?

It may be that the warm feeling of positive self-regard you felt in the yoga class, which you had hoped would last all day, vanished suddenly at the stoplight. It's not clear to you at that moment why you feel waves of sadness, worry, and discontent. An emptiness, a feeling of not fitting in, of being useless. Could it have something to do with catching sight of the human being at your window?

She's holding a piece of cardboard with the words "HUN-GRY and HOMELESS. I'm SOBER. Please HELP!"

The light turns green, and you're on your way.

Happiness isn't just personal. Being content implies aware-ness of the lives of others. Isn't it possible that if your community is vibrant and sustained, a more lasting and comprehensive feeling of well-being will become part of your self-awareness and identity?

Ukeireru is an awareness of others and an acceptance of their vulnerabilities. It alleviates the tension of feeling that the pursuit of happiness is the key to well-being. Ironically, it's the reverse: when we accept others and feel joined to them, more possibilities for well-being are created.

Our identities, thought to be personal, are established and maintained by the people around us and how they're living. Maybe the framers of the Constitution wouldn't have limited themselves to the pursuit of happiness had they accepted the responsibility for the injustices that they caused, perpetuated, and institutionalized and that contributed to their unhappiness and pursuit.

Whether we are consciously aware of it or not, when other human beings suffer, we cannot achieve well-being.

The World Health Organization estimates a rate of depression in Japan that is between 7 and 10 percent of the population. Even accounting for unreported mental illness, that's still less than half the rate of depression in the United States—19.2 percent. What may account for the differences is an outlook on life that is fundamentally Japanese.

Prior to the Meiji Restoration, when the "I" of the West was added to the "We" of Japan, there existed a different system of self-understanding and acceptance in Japan. That outlook, which can be described in many ways, including *ukeireru*, demonstrated what it means to be part of the group, part of society as a whole. Being an individual in Japan, for centuries before Western systems came to define many aspects of life there, was defined by groups.

This means trying to accept one's place in nature and community. It takes the pressure off figuring out one's purpose in life. That purpose is provided for and defined by the group. Whether it's one's ancestors, parents, spouse, community, or employer, being Japanese means that who you are is determined in large measure by others. The benefit of that, when it works, is *ukeireru*: being accepted, having a place in the world valued by nature and people.

The enormous challenge in Japan is how groups are defined. Historically, comparable to other societies, Japan remains a male-dominated collection of organizations. Countless articles appear in global media: low rates of women in executive positions in Japan, men unwilling in Japan to share family responsibilities, Japanese medical schools rejecting women applicants, companies refusing to hire married women or women with children. Lots more needs to be done for Japan to advance.

Western systems were needed to introduce concepts and methods of individual rights in Japan.

"Boys, be ambitious!" That's the motto of Hokkaido University, an institution founded by William Clark of Massachusetts in 1876. (Note the gender in the motto.) To this day in Japan, that slogan resonates, and ordinary Japanese know it. "Boys, be ambitious!" is also the name of a pop song and manga comic book.

Being ambitious, asserting one's individuality, was literally a foreign concept. The postwar Japanese constitution is also foreign; some of its articles introduced Western laws.

Beate Sirota Gordon and Eleanor Hadley, two Americans, wrote the articles in the constitution relating to civil rights. Thanks to these two women, the Japanese constitution includes articles 14 and 24 on Equal Rights and Women's Civil Rights. Article 14 states, "All of the people are equal under the law and there shall be no discrimination in political, economic or social relations because of race, creed, sex, social status or family origin." Article 24 states, "(1) Marriage shall be based only on the mutual consent of both sexes and it shall be maintained through mutual cooperation with the equal rights of husband and wife as a basis. (2) With regard to choice of spouse, property rights, inheritance, choice of domicile, divorce and other matters pertaining to marriage and the family, laws shall be enacted from the standpoint of individual dignity and the essential equality of the sexes."

So, truth be told, if I was writing this book primarily for Japanese, I'd be telling people all about the importance of challenging conformity.

I've had many conversations with friends in Japan and listened to their frustrations with feeling the pressure to conform to the standards and ideals of groups that place demands on them. These demands ride roughshod over their innermost desires. Breaking away from the group norms can cause shame, sadness, worrying, and isolation.

But when we are primarily concerned *here* about our own happiness, whatever leads to it becomes the focus. That's fine. Yoga, mindfulness, and meditation are wonderful ways to alleviate stress.

If it stops there, however, if there isn't enough of a component or recognition of others' needs, the sources of unhappiness are not being addressed adequately. And they go on and on and on.

I'm not saying your efforts toward self-acceptance should only be about the economics that contribute to mental illness. What I *am* saying is that you should take the calm—not the happiness—that comes from accepting yourself and your place in nature, and think about or even do something about what made you miserable and scared in the first place.

Take a look at this recent announcement from the Massachusetts Psychological Association about an upcoming conference:

Acceptance and Commitment Therapy (ACT) is an evidence-based, transdiagnostic, contextual behavioral treatment approach that can be used across myriad mental health issues. Treatment targets include experiential avoidance and cognitive fusion, found to be central to mood and anxiety disorders. ACT employs acceptance/mindfulness and valued action/commitment processes to increase clients' ability to increase psychological flexibility. ACT developed from a robust empirical base exploring basic verbal processes (i.e., Relational Frame Theory) and has been evaluated in close to 250 clinical trials, suggesting its efficacy across numerous psychological disorders, including anxiety, chronic pain, OCD, depression, psychosis, smoking cessation, stress, burnout, and parenting.

But what *causes* the stress and the burnout?

Like happiness, stress isn't just personal. Just as Japan abandoned feudalism and became a modern nation, we would benefit here from fixing systems, institutions, and relationships that pit us against one another. The late nineteenth century demanded that Japan develop institutions that valued individualism needed to create and compete with the world and that it include all sorts of people in decision making, not just feudal lords or priests and monks. The twenty-first century demands that the West increasingly develop approaches that value acceptance of others and lead to changing systems and institutions that cause stress.

Aim for well-being that provides the clarity needed to make decisions about your life and those who need your help. When we're stressed out, we make poor decisions, no doubt about it. We act impulsively, without thinking, barely aware of the consequences, mostly disregarding the impact of what we are doing to the group or other person. It becomes instead an urgent situation, escalating into a crisis or even emergency. While you might win the argument or get what you're after through your aggression, you've also made yourself and others miserable and stressed out.

That misery and stress don't go away. They become the foundation for the next conflict and the next dramatic display.

When we're calm, we can choose to act or not act.

Because the West is made up of heterogeneous nations, rich in diversity, applying *ukeireru* here has the potential to *add* meaning to our lives. We can balance our relentless celebration of and preoccupation with the individual by accepting the numerous groups in which we find ourselves. Just as Japanese grew and changed for the better by adopting Western ways, so, too, can we benefit from taking on some of their approaches. It's not one or the other; it's not about which system is best. Neither is ideal. It's about creating change in our lives by adding what's missing and doing away with tactics and strategies that perpetuate conflicts.

That 19.2 percent rate of depression in the United States is a big number. You'd think that the pursuit of happiness would have a better outcome. Something's wrong. It's not just the sheer exhaustion of pursuing happiness, nor is it loneliness.

The suffering around you is eroding your sense of well-being. It's unavoidable, even in gated communities, even if you tell yourself that you deserve to be happy, and even if you feel entitled to all your stuff. We are an empathic species, hardwired for caring and for accepting others, and when we witness suffering, which is all around us, we suffer, too.

Chapter
Sixteen

Revisiting Acceptance

I can pinpoint the moment when it occurred to me that Japan might be a way out of my stress. The movie was *Rashomon*, and I had just entered adolescence. The world was black or white.

My parents were completely wrong, or they were 100 percent correct. A problem had one solution, or if there appeared to be more than one, then only one solution was the best; the other possibilities had no value.

Along comes *Rashomon*.

It's Saturday night, summertime, and Channel 13 is running a weekly series of classic movies: *Jules and Jim*, *The 400 Blows*, *The Rules of the Game*, *The Virgin Spring*, *Potemkin*, and others, all European, except for *Rashomon*.

Toshiro Mifune, as *Tajōmaru*, the bad guy, bound with ropes, in a loincloth, not only squirms and wriggles against the ropes but laughs in the face of his accusers, groans, shows rage, raw power, a lack of restraint. He is a force of nature.

Man oh man!

He's accused of a crime, captured and tied up, but so indifferent to his fate that he remains defiant. He just doesn't care.

Who else?

There's a dead samurai (whose story is told through a medium), his wife, a priest, a villager, a judge, and a woodcutter. The samurai's wife was raped by the outlaw. Or was she? What happened? Did the samurai kill himself? Or was he killed by *Tajōmaru*? The characters tell their stories, which are contradictory or inconsistent. If you put them together, side by side, you get different narratives that don't add up.

What I learned was that each point of view has its own element of truth, not a truth that will lead to a conviction, and not a truth acceptable to others who were there, but a truth. And that truth is part of a group and a way of seeing things or a recognition that each person holds on to their version of what took place, which may be at extreme odds with others. But somehow everyone accepts the narratives as parts of a whole.

It was an incredibly liberating thought, and though for sure I have no idea how deeply it entered and developed in my pea brain of early teen years, I know it had enormous impact. Even if I did not have the words or awareness back then, something took place after watching that movie that had not occurred before.

The movie meant to me that whatever it was I felt or thought, feelings and thoughts often contrary to those of my parents, was valid. I was a real person with my own standards.

My mother and father laid down the law. They told me what it was I was feeling. I was animated by them. I didn't know who I was or what I felt unless they told me. But after watching that movie, I figured I had my own point of view. I was young enough to experience this as a revelation.

The bad guy's point of view wasn't admirable, but even though he was a bad guy, and he was, he had an outlook that the other characters had to accept. They had to deal with him. He couldn't be ignored. As *Tajōmaru* tells his story, his version of what took place, Kurosawa, the director, *shows* you his story. It's convincing.

My highly personal, very adolescent view of *Rashomon* seems kind of bizarre as I look back on it from so many years' distance. I mean, really? *Rashomon* as a story about accepting one's true identity? Seriously?

But what I took from it was this: if I was to tell people about life in my home, some incident that had taken place, my version of events would be different from those of my parents. Not a bad place to start when trying to accept who you are as a person.

Anyway, good or bad, it's where I started.

Children who grow up in abusive homes often live in their heads, are inventive, and come up with lots of solid reasons for the abuse. That way there is order. Our species loves order.

Another thing about abusive homes is that, after a while, families get used to the abuse, it becomes a way of life, a cult, in which outsiders are seen as disruptive.

Excuses are made for the abusive parent; questions that arise from people outside of the family are regarded as intrusions or even threats.

The family develops a shared narrative—a version of events that keeps them together and binds them to one another. Their intimacy is exclusive, defining, and a key part of their identity as individuals within the group. Leaving the group means a loss of identity, which can be terrifying.

This adhesive bond explains why people who break free of abusive families are often plagued by doubts, guilt, and a sense of betrayal. Not only have they lost who they were, a loss that creates loneliness, they have also betrayed the family. It's one reason, among many, that people from abusive families can wind up in abusive marriages: home, sweet home.

And even for those who had the great, good fortune to have avoided abuse, knowing others who have had that experience, working with them, listening to their music, watching them perform, being in intimate relationships with them, and reading their books? That contact, artistic and emotional, means that the experiences of the abused inform those who got off easy.

That's what empathy and relationships do: make it clear that who you are depends heavily on others.

Certain sayings were repeated when I was growing up. If you didn't go along with these, fought back by offering your version, you could, and here is another saying, *"Have your head handed to you."*

Here are a few key sayings I heard often:

"Other families don't fight as much as ours because they don't love one another as much."

"If I don't tell you how I feel, how will you know?"

"I had a fantasy of what this weekend would be like, and you disappointed me."

"I only hope and pray that one day my son will come back to me, but by then it will be too late. I'll be dead and gone."

A few weeks after watching *Rashomon*, I went to Paperback Booksmith on Front Street, across from the Liberty Theatre and down the street from the YWCA, and bought books by Japanese writers.

I had no idea whose works to read and chose authors whose names were Japanese. The books also had to be short, under two hundred pages, as my attention span and ability to absorb and concentrate and remember what I was reading were very limited at that time.

I was distracted those days and nights by just about everything, reactive and judgmental, so consumed by fear that I was used to being afraid and thought others were as afraid as me. I was so afraid I didn't even know I was afraid.

I didn't know that the rage and madness in my home were not ordinary. I had no experience with any forms of intimacy other than what I had with my mother and father and sister.

Snow Country, by Yasunari Kawabata, was the first book I read by a Japanese writer. Its opening sentence is famous in Japan: "The train came out of the long tunnel into the snow country."

Then I read *Thousand Cranes*, also by Kawabata. I still have that book, in which I underlined:

> *The red sun seemed about to flow down over the branches.*
> *The grove stood dark against it.*
> *The sun flowing over the branches sank into his tired eyes, and he closed them.*
> *The white cranes from the Inamura girl's kerchief flew across the evening sun, which was still in his eyes.*

Other books around the same time: *The Sailor Who Fell from Grace with the Sea* and *Death in Midsummer*, novels by Yukio Mishima. I read Tanizaki. *Some Prefer Nettles* is his short novel about an unhappy marriage. At the age of fourteen, I underlined this sentence: "You have to be careful with children—some day they grow up."

As I got older, I maintained interest in Japan but didn't read many books about the country or see a lot of Japanese movies. This was way before Japan came to occupy an inspiring role in contemporary life in the United States. People back then still saw "Made in Japan" as a sign of cheap goods, and associations with Japan centered around words like

"Pearl Harbor," "geisha girls," "Hiroshima," "sumo wrestling," and "samurai." Sushi didn't exist in the States (except in a few elite restaurants and Japanese or Korean homes), and ramen was unheard of. We did have Benihana!

In 2003, just before I left for my first trip to Japan, I had phoned everyone I knew who might know someone in Japan, or who had been to Japan, and through this little network I first met Yuko and Shinji.

It was November, cloudy and cool, and light rain fell on our walks through Yoyogi Park. We stood beside canals. I had *shochu* in a renovated artist's studio in the middle of nowhere. It was some remote neighborhood—I took a taxi there, have no idea how to find it again. We visited book stalls filled with old volumes.

Mostly we were together; it was a new kind of intimacy, whether with friends or not, and a lot of looking took place. Looking at how she held chopsticks. Looking at how he drank from a cup of barley tea.

My friends spoke fluent English, but a lot went on without words—that was my first experience of something like that! It felt strange and awkward to gesture about where to sit or to ask for something, but it wasn't long before I preferred the silence to speech. I felt soothed and understood. I didn't *want* words. They didn't need to tell me how they felt because I knew. It was my first experience of *ukeireru*.

Subsequent trips to Japan, twenty-eight since that first visit, took me to homes, schools, shrines, temples, jazz clubs, rave clubs, cafés, hot springs inns, forests, mountaintops, oceans, lakes, rivers, offices, apartments, factories, farms, and conferences.

I am hired to work and speak in Japan and to write about the country for Western and Japanese companies and media.

The owner of an inn on Awaji Island took me to a Shinto shrine and organized a purification ceremony in which I participated and felt cleansed afterward.

A friend allowed me to walk Chocolate, his beautiful brown Labrador retriever, along the brook below his home, where Bashō had composed poetry centuries earlier.

In Niigata I gave a talk at a conference: "Sushi: Is It the Pizza of the Twenty-First Century?"

In Shizuoka prefecture, a farmer and I drank green tea while he spoke of the hardships of getting the next generation to take over the farm.

Yakushima Island, south of Kyushu, filled my heart as I walked with my wife through the ancient cedar forests that inspired Hayao Miyazaki, the director of the anime movie *Princess Mononoke*.

No matter where I go in Japan, experiences take place that become memorable: the ways in which people try to join nature, to suss out their place in it, to accept others through emotion that's unspoken.

The Japan I visit isn't like the one shown in *Rashomon*. How could it be? Expecting that would be like a Japanese going to Mexico after seeing *The Treasure of the Sierra Madre* and imagining that it would look like that movie.

Maybe that's not so far-fetched. Both movies were made soon after the Second World War had ended, *The Treasure of the Sierra Madre* in 1948 and *Rashomon* in 1950. They share these questions:

What does it mean to be a human being?

How do we preserve the things that make us most human in the face of tragedy?

Why are we motivated by greed and selfishness?

So, yes, alongside the lyricism and acceptance of Japan, the worship of nature, I see degradation, cruelty, and emotional confinement. Group cohesion can erode or destroy individualism and creativity. Those without social authority can be kept disenfranchised by the group. Acceptance can be misused and serve as a cudgel to try to force people to resign themselves to institutions and systems.

It's similar to being part of a family. At its best, a family— a mother and a child—demonstrate silent communication and acceptance. At its worst, a family convinces children that their dreams and aspirations are meaningless.

How can there be such disparate experiences from the same source?

My father was brought up in foster homes in New York City during his teen years. He didn't find out until years later what happened to his parents and sister and brother.

I can only imagine the deep silences he dwelled in while awaiting word.

Not a word. Can you imagine being that child?

From the age of fourteen until he was nineteen, he didn't know that his parents and sister had been murdered. His brother survived incarceration.

He had had hope. He was that young. He had had doubts. Hope and doubt overwhelmed him. He was confused and disoriented.

I wonder what language he thought in when he thought of his family. Where they were, what they were doing, if they were living. Or dead. Of how they died.

He made things up and told me that he received letters from them long after no communication was possible on their end. Just silence, just what he had of them in his heart, or *Kuuki wo yomu*. Waiting.

My family were German Jews who had lived in Bavaria for centuries: livestock traders, innkeepers, textile merchants. My grandfather was a war veteran who was wounded in 1917 fighting in France for Germany. These were rarely matters ever mentioned in my home.

Are resilient Japanese traditions of acceptance a reaction to trauma of war and history? Do I feel a connection to Japan because of that?

I don't know. I do know this:

It's not about being happy. It's about learning to live with disappointment, making others safe, and developing insight that helps you understand that happiness flees when there is loss. What's lost must be accepted.

After all, why be happy when there is so much work that still needs to be done?

Acknowledgments

I can't imagine writing this book without the love, support, guidance, and insights of my wife, Laura. Similarly, my children, Madeline and Nicholas, are incomparable in allowing me to see the world through their eyes.

This book would never have seen the light of day had it not been for the steadfast faith and commitment of my agent, Michelle Tessler, whose patience should be bottled. My editor Renee Sedliar is literary royalty, as far as I'm concerned, capable of showing me where I went awry and how to get back to the story. Her entire team at Hachette Go has also been a real pleasure to work with and learn from, including Alison Dalafave and Amber Morris.

Friends and colleagues added a lot to my understanding: Jiro Takeuchi, Yuko Enomoto, Shinji Nohara, Takeshi Endo, Yukiko Kamiya, Mika Horie, Hiroshi Kagawa, Ken Yokoyama, Ignatius Cronin, Rie Oshima, Robb Satterwhite, Yumi Obinata, Rumiko Obata, Daniel Boulud, Taeko Takigami, Marian Goldberg, Georgette Farkas, Kobo Senju, Kazuhiko Kobayashi, John Gauntner, Lloyd Nakano, Nancy

Acknowledgments

Berliner, Izumi Nakagawa, Sachiko Nakamichi, Kazunari Nakamichi, Nozomi Obinata, Anri Yamazu, Kiyomi Tsurusawa, Kanna Izuka, Yuki Kojima, Yoko Nomura, and Tatsuya Sudo.

Special thanks to Selbsanft.

Bibliography

Adams, Tim. "Sherry Turkle: 'I Am Not Anti-Technology, I Am Pro-Conversation.'" *Guardian* (London), October 18, 2015.

Alemoru, Kemi. "Black Power Naps Is an Installation About the Power of Doing Nothing." Dazed. June 27, 2018. dazeddigital.com/art-photography/article/40506/1/black -power-naps-installation-reclaiming-rest.

Barthes, Roland. *Empire of Signs*. Translated by Richard Howard. New York: Hill and Wang, 1987.

Benjamin, Gail. *Japanese Lessons: A Year in a Japanese School Through the Eyes of an American Anthropologist and Her Children*. New York: New York University Press, 1997.

Berger, John. *Ways of Seeing*. New York: Penguin, 1972.

Bestor, Ted. *Neighborhood Tokyo*. Stanford, CA: Stanford University Press, 1989.

———. *Tsukiji: The Fish Market at the Center of the World*. Berkeley: University of California Press, 2004.

Brody, Jane. "The Secret to Good Health May Be a Walk in the Park." *New York Times*, December 3, 2018.

Buruma, Ian. *Inventing Japan*. New York: Modern Library, 2003.

Bibliography

Carter, Richard Burnett. *The Language of Zen: Heart Speaking to Heart*. New York: Ethos, 2010.

Cederström, Carl. *The Happiness Fantasy*. Cambridge, UK: Polity, 2018.

Cortazzi, Hugh. "The Curse of *Shikata Ga Nai*." *Japan Times,* April 16, 2001.

Crary, Jonathan. *24/7: Late Capitalism and the Ends of Sleep*. London: Verso, 2014.

Cwiertka, Katarzyna. *Modern Japanese Cuisine*. London: Reaktion Books, 2006.

Davies, Roger J., and Osamu Ikeno, editors. *The Japanese Mind: Understanding Contemporary Japanese Culture*. Boston: Tuttle, 2002.

Dazai, Osamu. *No Longer Human*. New York: New Directions, 1973.

Dogen. *How to Cook Your Life*. Boston: Shambhala Publications, 2005.

Doi, Takeo. *The Anatomy of Dependence*. New York: Kodansha, 1971.

Eddo-Lodge, Reni. *Why I'm No Longer Talking to White People About Race*. New York: Bloomsbury, 2019.

Galloway, Lindsey. "What It's Like to Live in a Well-Governed Country." BBC, January 8, 2018. bbc.com/travel/story/2018 0107-what-its-like-to-live-in-a-well-governed-country.

Genda, Yuji. *A Nagging Sense of Job Insecurity*. Tokyo: International House of Japan, 2005.

"A Good Night's Sleep Is Critical for Good Health." Press release. Centers for Disease Control and Prevention, February 18, 2016. cdc.gov/media/releases/2016/p0215-enough-sleep.html.

232

Griffiths, Sarah. "Can Decluttering Your House Really Make You Happier?" BBC, May 15, 2019. bbc.com/future/article /20190515-can-decluttering-your-house-really-spark-joy.

"Gross Domestic Product (GDP) (Indicator)." OECD. data.oecd .org/gdp/gross-domestic-product-gdp.htm. Accessed December 18, 2019.

Haas, Scott. "Hashiri, Sakari, Nagori: Toward Understanding the Psychology, Ideology, and Branding of Seasonality in Japanese Gastronomy." *Gastronomica: The Journal of Critical Food Studies* 15, no. 2 (Summer 2015).

———. "Kenny Garrett: One-of-a-Kind." *Bay State Banner* (Boston), August 29, 2019.

———. "The Price of Harmony: The Ideology of Japanese Cuisine." *Gastronomica: The Journal of Critical Food Studies* 17, no. 2 (Summer 2017).

———. *Those Immigrants! Indians in America: A Psychological Exploration of Achievement*. New Delhi: Fingerprint, 2016.

Han, Byung-Chul. *The Burnout Society*. Translated by Erik Butler. Stanford, CA: Stanford University Press, 2015.

Hashimoto, Akiko. *The Long Defeat*. New York: Oxford University Press, 2015.

Hirata, Keiko, and Mark Waschauer. *Japan: The Paradox of Harmony*. New Haven, CT: Yale University Press, 2014.

"Inside Google Workplaces, from Perks to Nap Pods." CBS News, January 22, 2013.

Ishinomori, Shotaro. *Japan, Inc.* Berkeley: University of California Press, 1988.

Isozaki, Arata. *Japan-ness in Architecture*. Cambridge, MA: MIT Press, 2011.

Ito, Shingo. "Stop It! Tokyo Police Anti-Groper App Becomes Smash Hit in Japan." *Japan Times,* May 23, 2019. japantimes .co.jp/news/2019/05/23/national/social-issues/stop-tokyo -police-anti-groper-app-becomes-smash-hit-japan.

Iyer, Pico. *Autumn Light.* New York: Knopf, 2019.

"Japanese Firms Starting to Encourage Employees to Take Naps at Work." *Japan Times,* November 22, 2018.

Japan Rising: The Iwakura Embassy to the USA and Europe 1871– 1873. Compiled by Kume Kunitake and edited by Chushichi Tsuzuki and R. Jule Young. New York: Cambridge University Press, 2009.

"Japan's Farming Population Rapidly Aging and Decreasing." Nippon.com, July 3, 2018. nippon.com/en/features/h00227 /japan's-farming-population-rapidly-aging-and-decreasing .html.

Kawabata, Yasunari. *Beauty and Sadness.* Translated by Howard Hibbett. New York: Vintage, 1996.

———. *Snow Country.* Translated by Edward Seidensticker. New York: Berkley Medallion, 1968.

———. *Thousand Cranes.* Translated by Edward Seidensticker. New York: Berkley Medallion, 1968.

Kawai, Hayao. *Buddhism and the Art of Psychotherapy.* College Station: Texas A&M University Press, 1996.

Kawai, Hayao, and Murakami, Haruki. *Haruki Murakami Goes to Meet Hayao Kawai.* Translated by Christopher Stephens. Einsiedeln, Switzerland: Daimon Publishers, 2016.

Keene, Donald. *Modern Japanese Diaries.* New York: Henry Holt, 1995.

Kenkō, Yoshida. *Essays in Idleness.* Translated by Donald Keene. New York: Columbia University Press, 1967.

Kurosawa, Akira. *Something Like an Autobiography.* New York: Vintage, 1983.

Lebra, Takie Sugiyama. *Japanese Patterns of Behavior.* Honolulu: University of Hawaii Press, 1976.

Levin, Marc, director. *One Nation Under Stress.* HBO Documentary Films, 2019.

Lewis-Stempel, John. *The Secret Life of the Owl.* London: Transworld Publishers, 2017.

Lifton, Robert Jay. *Death in Life.* New York: Vintage Books, 1969.

MacDonald, Helen. *H is for Hawk.* London: Jonathan Cape, 2014.

Maier, Corinne. *Bonjour Laziness.* New York: Pantheon, 2005.

Mantel, Hilary. *Giving Up the Ghost.* Picador: New York, 2003.

Mathews, Gordon. *What Makes Life Worth Living? How Japanese and Americans Make Sense of Their Worlds.* Berkeley: University of California Press, 1996.

Mautz, Scott. "Lack of Sleep Is (Literally) Killing You: Here's Why and What to Do, According to Science." scottmautz.com/lack-of-sleep-is-literally-killing-you-heres-why-and-what-to-do-according-to-science.

McCurry, Justin. "Japanese Firms Encourage Their Dozy Workers to Sleep on the Job," *Guardian* (London), August 18, 2014. theguardian.com/world/2014/aug/18/japanese-firms-encourage-workers-sleep-on-job.

Minami, Hiroshi. *Psychology of the Japanese People.* Toronto: University of Toronto Press, 1971.

Mishima, Yukio. *Confessions of a Mask*. Translated by John Nathan. New York: New Directions, 1958.

———. *Death in Midsummer*. Translated by John Nathan. New York: Penguin, 1973.

———. *The Sailor Who Fell from Grace with the Sea*. Translated by John Nathan. Great Britain: Penguin, 1973.

Morita, Shoma. *Morita Therapy and the True Nature of Anxiety-Based Disorders*. Albany: SUNY Press, 1998.

Nakamura, Karen. *A Disability of the Soul*. Ithaca, NY: Cornell University Press, 2012.

Nakane, Chie. *Japanese Society*. Berkeley: University of California Press, 1970.

Nathan, John. *Living Carelessly in Japan and Elsewhere*. New York: Free Press, 2008.

Ohnuki-Tierney, Emiko. *Rice as Self: Japanese Identities Through Time*. Princeton, NJ: Princeton University Press, 1993.

Pilling, David. *The Growth Delusion*. New York: Crown, 2018.

Qin, Amy. "Pritzker Prize Goes to Arata Isozaki, Designer for a Postwar World." *New York Times*, March 5, 2019.

Rath, Eric. *Japan's Cuisines*. London: Reaktion, 2016.

Redfield, Robert R. "CDC Director's Media Statement on U.S. Life Expectancy." CDC Newsroom. November 29, 2018. cdc .gov/media/releases/2018/s1129-US-life-expectancy.html.

Reischauer, Edwin, and Marius Jansen. *The Japanese Today: Change and Continuity*. Cambridge, MA: Belknap of Harvard University Press, 2001.

Reynolds, David K. *The Quiet Therapies: Japanese Pathways to Personal Growth*. Honolulu: University of Hawaii Press, 1980.

Reynolds, Gretchen. "Loneliness Is Bad for Your Health; An App May Help." *New York Times*, February 20, 2019.

Ro, Christine. "When the Going Gets Tough, Have a Nap." BBC, October 9, 2018. bbc.com/future/article/20181009 -how-sleep-helps-with-emotional-recovery-and-trauma.

Robertson, Jennifer. *Robo Sapiens Japanicus: Robots, Gender, Family, and the Japanese Nation.* Oakland, California: University of California Press, 2017.

Rogers, Krista. "A Brief History of the Evolution of Japanese School Lunches." *Japan Today*, January 14, 2015. japan today.com/category/features/food/a-brief-history-of-the -evolution-of-japanese-school-lunches.

Rohlen, Thomas P. *Japan's High Schools.* Berkeley: University of California Press, 1983.

Sacks, Oliver. *Everything in Its Place: First Loves and Last Tales.* New York: Knopf, 2019.

Saga, Junichi. *Memories of Silk and Straw: A Self-Portrait of Small-Town Japan.* Translated by Garry O. Evans. Tokyo: Kodansha, 1990.

Saxbe, Darby E., and Rena Repetti. "No Place Like Home: Home Tours Correlate with Daily Patterns of Mood and Cortisol." *Personality and Social Psychology Bulletin*, November 23, 2009.

"Shiki Soku Zeku Ku Soku Ze Shiki." Form Is Itself Voidness. May 26, 2013. shikisokuzekw.tumblr.com/post/513656498 57/shiki-soku-zeku-ku-soku-ze-shiki.

sleep.org. "Sleeping at Work: Companies with Nap Rooms and Snooze-Friendly Policies." sleep.org/articles/sleeping-work -companies-nap-rooms-snooze-friendly-policies.

Smil, Vaclav, and Kazuhiko Kobayashi. *Japan's Dietary Transition and Its Impacts*. Cambridge, MA: MIT Press, 2012.

Smith, Tiffany Watt. *Schadenfreude*. London: Wellcome Collection, 2018.

Sōseki, Natsume. *Botchan*. Translated by J. Cohn. New York: Penguin, 2012.

Stokes, Henry Scott. *The Life and Death of Yukio Mishima*. New York: Farrar, Straus and Giroux, 1974.

Sugiyama, Kotaro, and Timothy Andree. *The Dentsu Way*. New York: McGraw-Hill, 2011.

"Suicide Rate by Country Population." World Population Review. August 27, 2019. worldpopulationreview.com/countries /suicide-rate-by-country.

Suzuki, D. T. *Zen and Japanese Culture*. Princeton, NJ: Princeton University Press, 2010.

Tanizaki, Jun'ichirō. *In Praise of Shadows*. Translated by Thomas J. Harper. Sedgwick, ME: Leete's Island Books, 1977.

———. *The Makioka Sisters*. Translated by Edward Seidensticker. New York: Vintage, 1995.

———. *Some Prefer Nettles*. Translated by Edward Seidensticker. New York: Vintage, 1970.

Turkle, Sherry. *Reclaiming Conversation: The Power of Talk in a Digital Age*. New York: Penguin, 2015.

Watanabe, Hiroshi. *The Architecture of Tokyo*. Stuttgart, Germany: Edition Axel Menges, 2001.

White, Merry. *Coffee Life in Japan*. Berkeley, CA: University of California Press, 2012.

Wohlleben, Peter. *The Hidden Life of Trees*. Translated by Jane Billinghurst. Vancouver, Canada: Greystone Books, 2015.

Yamakuse, Yoji. *Japaneseness: A Guide to Values and Virtues.* Translated by Michael A. Cooney. Berkeley, CA: Stone Bridge Press, 2016.

Yokoyama, Hideo. *Six-Four.* Translated by Jonathan Lloyd Davies. London: Riverrun, 2016.

Young, Rosamund. *The Secret Life of Cows.* New York: Penguin, 2018.